Good Morning, Gugal-Dong!

And Other Stories to Read on the John

Dallas Thomas

Illustration by Steve Robinson

CONTENTS

BOOK INTRODUCTION

In the last 10 years, I've worn two professional hats: school teacher and psychotherapist. In the last three years, I've hung up the teaching hat and worked exclusively in therapy and mental health.

Back when I was a teacher, I learned very quickly that one of the best ways to engage a classroom full of students was to tell them a short story that captured their attention and made them laugh. This was a great way to keep their focus, build rapport and reduce behaviour challenges. As a substitute teacher who visited many different classrooms, grades and schools, I frequently shared unique stories with the students I met.

As a psychotherapist, I spend the better part of my days listening to people's stories, while providing them with tools and insights that will hopefully equip them to better navigate their pain and problems. On most days, I get the honoured privilege of hearing people share their deeply personal accounts of life. Due to the strict limits of confidentiality and a desire to protect my clients, I'm unable to share their stories.

It's a unique job in that sense, where I hear some of the most compelling and vulnerable stories I will ever hear, yet will never be able to share any of them. This is unlike any other job where one might come home and tell everyone ALL the details of how the day went.

Listening to their stories is sometimes quite heavy and tragic. One of the ways I cope with this is to try and incorporate humour into my days, doing things that make me laugh as often as is acceptable (and sometimes unacceptable).

It's a grounding experience for me to find humour and joy in the mundane matters of life, and I spend a lot of time observing people and situations purely for this reason. Observing people makes me laugh and laughter triggers the release of endorphins, the body's natural "feel-good" chemicals. Endorphins promote an overall sense of well-being and can even temporarily relieve pain. Finding the humour in things really is the best medicine.

There are stories everywhere you look, if you look in the right way. This is my collection of short stories and commentary from situations I have witnessed over the years. Some of them are touching, others are silly and most are absurd.

It is my sincere hope that these stories add a little bit of joy to your days and make you laugh. There is also the chance that you may finish reading these stories and conclude that the author needs therapy himself. I can assure you, I am already seeing my own therapist.

GOOD MORNING, GUGAL-DONG!
~ For Paul H. ~

I've always been someone who pushes myself. Whether it's writing this book, opening up my psychotherapy practice, or taking on a new hobby, I am continuously in pursuit of trying new things I find meaningful.

As I went for a run this evening, I was reminded of when I was living in Korea and I pushed myself to be in the best shape of my life.

I lived in a "village" called Gugal-dong. I say "village" because really, Gugal-dong was more of a dim, comatose town. In fact, the name of the town couldn't be more unoriginal: it was literally named after the Google Homepage (*Gugal* meaning Google, *Dong* meaning town). Gugal-dong had a University called Kangnam, a few little apartment complexes that all looked the same and a Buddhist temple amongst a large number of various Christian churches.

Other than some small mountains on the outskirts, the landscape left much to be desired. In the spring, the cherry blossoms would bloom and enhance the drab looking buildings for a few weeks, then they'd go back to looking dull and grey. Korea was rapidly built in the span of a few decades after the Korean War ended, and this was reflected in how quickly they put up buildings without much thought towards how they looked. Korea has many things going for it, but architecture is not one of them.

While my apartment building was bleak on the outside, on the inside it was streamlined and high-tech. The entrance to my tiny

3

apartment suite was adorned with this shiny metal Star Trek-esque lock. This lock required a series of meticulous steps to decode it, reminding me of the Starship motherboard. After carefully entering my combination, I would eagerly await the *click* and *whoosh* notifying me of success. In addition to an unnecessarily sophisticated lock, my apartment included a tiny bed, heated floors, a little table that required me to sit cross-legged on the floor and a toilet with way too many buttons.

I worked from 12 pm - 9 pm, Monday to Friday, teaching English to kids who had just spent an entire day at school, were tired, and not too interested in what I had to say. Each kid in my school was allowed to give themselves their own English name. The majority of the boys in my class called themselves Harry because Harry Potter was the big thing at the time. Most of the girls were called "Sue" and one child wanted to be called "Optimus Prime." Every second day, I would have to call Optimus on the phone, refer to him as such, and chat with him in English to encourage his communication skills.

I only knew a handful of English teachers and even though I was surrounded by people, I often felt alone. It's a weird feeling. I could hear anything and everything through the thin walls of my apartment and was never more than a few meters away from someone, yet I never got to know any of my neighbours.

At the recommendation of a fellow English teacher, I joined the community "Google Town Gym". My goal was to get in peak condition to prepare myself for climbing Seoraksan Mountain later that Fall.

Since most kids were in school and most adults were at work, I was in the gym early every morning surrounded by retired Korean people. Now, there is something you should know about elderly Koreans: they are nothing like your typical North American seniors. In Korea, it is not uncommon to see old ladies and old men in their 80's and 90's working out all the time. And, if they aren't exercising in the gym, you can often spot really old Korean people hiking in the mountains or using randomly placed workout equipment in the forests. How they get this equipment in the forest is beyond me. Then, there's the workout attire. Not only are these Korean seniors working out in eccentric places, but their getup is something else. Regardless of the time, activity or setting, they always seem to be wearing tracksuits of some kind, as well as large head visors to shield their skin from the sun. In Korea, there is an odd fear of the sun and its damage to the skin, which is funny because it was foggy so often.

The guy who oversaw the gym was called Mr. Kim. He was ripped. He had won weightlifting competitions in the past and there was a poster of him in his glory days next to his little desk that said, "Mr. Korea". He didn't speak a word of English nor did he seem interested in trying. Mr. Kim sported sweatpants, a low cut shirt and hair so messy that it looked like he hadn't consulted a mirror in days. Every day Mr. Kim sat at the computer near the gym entrance watching YouTube videos and laughing, indifferent to the activity around him.

Upon entering the gym, you'd see old Korean ladies doing undignified stretches and using machines in what could only be described as definitely the wrong way to use them. The older men would be doing a walkabout tour of the various workout stations, watching the Korean television set that was playing K-Pop in the background, while seemingly having no intention to workout themselves. If they did, it was very light circuits and stretches.

I was pretty disciplined at first. For the first few months, I'd wake up early in the morning, eat rice and kimchi, go to the gym, do pull-ups, pushups, bicep curls, run on the treadmill and bench press. I had a plan that I had set to follow, and from day one these old men would try to tell me that I was using the equipment incorrectly. Every single day. There were mirrors everywhere, and any time I was doing pull-ups or lifting weights, I could see them shaking their heads in disappointment, commenting to each other in Korean while pointing at me. They would then come by, try to move my hands to correct positions and/or would kick me off the station to model for me how to use it. Each time I would try to copy them, and they'd just shake their heads at me. Sometimes, the old ladies off to the side would watch us and laugh. Meanwhile, Mr. Korea sat at his desk watching YouTube, paying no attention to what was going on.

This scene played out every single morning, without fail. At first, I wasn't sure what to make of these old guys since the only interaction I had with them was either in the change room (where they could be found blow-drying both their heads and their groins) or inside the gym (where they were "critiquing" my form with great gusto).

After several weeks of the same scenario playing out, these old guys slowly started to welcome me into their world. They started to become more chatty, and while they still made fun of me, they began inviting me to spend time with them outside of the gym. They invited me to Korean BBQs at their homes, drinks out at pubs, hikes in the mountains, and fishing outings on the river. As we embarked on adventures together, through fragments of broken English I began learning about these men and developing a friendship with them.

One guy was a former police officer whose wife passed away. One guy was a former teacher whose life was now all about his grandkids. One guy ran his own convenience store, and my favourite was a guy called "Steve" whose job was to purchase high tech missile technology to defend against North Korea, in the event that they ever went to war. Steve told me he would soon retire and live in a cottage in the mountains where he could fish all day.

These men welcomed me into their world and made me their friend. They taught me the value of family, they taught me the virtue of silence, they taught me to never make assumptions about others. And while they couldn't offer me any valuable insight on how to do a bench press, the things I learned from them were priceless.

DON'T EAT THE YELLOW JON SNOW
~ For Ben K. ~

My wife's grandparents on her father's side are from Scotland. But, her father grew up in the city of Wolverhampton in England, and she grew up in Bath, so she considers herself English. Trev, my father-in-law, is English or Scottish depending on the accent he chooses to use in the moment. From my point of view he is English, not Scottish because a) he doesn't have red hair and b) I can understand him when he talks. Hannah's AncestryDNA results stated that most of her kin can be traced to Scotland.

My AncestryDNA results show that I'm 60% Ukrainian, then German, sprinkled with a little bit of Scandinavian. (Fun fact: after I wrote this story, in a strange twist of events, my AncestryDNA somehow updated my heritage to now include 2% Scottish heritage). Despite my lack of (ample) British heritage, I have been a longtime fan of Laphroaig, an Islay Single Malt Scotch Whisky which is made on the south coast of the island of Islay.

Legend has it that whiskey came to the British Isles by early Christian monks who had spent time in the Middle East and the Mediterranean where they learned the art of distilling. Celtic monks used to refer to it as *Aqua Vitae* meaning, Water of Life. I'd say that slowly sipping it borderlines on a mystical experience. If you have never had the pleasure of sipping Laphroaig scotch, allow me to enlighten you on the experience: when you first unscrew the sleek glass bottle, it's as though you are being kicked in the nostrils with the overpowering aroma of ash, oak and seaweed. After you swallow the burning liquid, the inside of your throat catches fire and once it settles in your belly, your body is forced into a state of deep relaxation and contemplation.

This scotch was first introduced to me by my brother-in-law when I lived in England. He offered me a small amount to cure a bad flu, and boy did it work. In less than ten minutes, my insides felt like they were kicking and my runny nose and congested chest cleared right up. In addition to an olfactory workout, when you purchase a bottle of Scottish imported Laphroaig, it comes with a small green document that is actually a lease on a square foot of land with the purchase of each bottle. If you follow their instructions you can register your name on this portion of land. So, technically... I own some land in Scotland on account of my (many) Laphroaig purchases.

One of my oldest friends, Ben Kennedy, can trace his father's side of the family back to the Kennedy clan in Scotland. Ben is convinced that there is a castle in Scotland that somehow belongs to him by lineage. He has yet to prove it though, but he is committed to claiming it for himself.

I wanted to lay this foundation to tell you about another famous foundation that stretches from the North Sea to the Irish Sea that was built by the Romans to keep out the invading Northmen who posed a threat to Roman expansion into the south. If you are a history buff, you will know that I'm talking about Hadrian's Wall.

Several years ago, Ben and I did a trip to Scotland, on a mission to find Hadrian's Wall. We flew from Toronto to London and then rented a car to drive from London up to Scotland. I distinctly remember renting the car because we had to drive on the left-hand side of the road and we almost died in the first 30 minutes, when Ben tried to merge onto the motorway. After that terrifying moment, all feelings of jet lag quickly left my body.

It can take a good six hours to drive from London to Scotland. We drove, and we drove, and we drove, and the farther north we went, the more beautiful it became. There were rolling hills of lush green countryside, dotted with sheep and stone hedge walls for many miles. Once we got closer to Scotland we were surrounded by hills and more mountains with expansive lakes and lochs. This drive was far more impressive than driving through my homeland, the

Prairies of Canada, where you can drive the same distance and see the same thing for the entire six hours: flat fields and blue sky.

Ben and I are both history enthusiasts, and our goal was to at least get to Hadrian's Wall before the sun set. We got lost several times, but as J.R.R. Tolkien says, "Not all who wander are lost." and that could not be truer when you are on an adventure where the journey itself is greater than the arrival to your destination. Our GPS in the car was not great (and this was before Google Maps) so our navigation guidance was limited. After hours of driving, we knew we were close to our destination and I was constantly looking out the window for any sign of this wall that the Romans had built.

Historians say Hadrian's Wall was commissioned by the Roman emperor Hadrian, who was born roughly 40 years after Jesus' death, and just a few years after the apostles Peter and Paul were executed in Rome. In 122 AD, Emperor Hadrian initiated the construction of a wall in Britannia to separate the civilized Romans from the barbarians to the north. Today, we know those "barbarians" were the Scotts, or Picts. It would take six years to build the wall and took the work of 15,000 men (three Roman legions). The sad thing is, Hadrian would never return to Britannia to see its completion. Soldiers from as far away as Syria came to work on the wall. The wall is 73 miles long and had soldiers from all parts of the Roman Empire garrisoned at its outposts.

For me, being able to visit the wall and put my hands on it, was like being able to go back in time 2,000 years ago, and that was a great part of the excitement. What if one of the soldiers stationed at the wall had seen or known Christians from the earliest of churches? What if some of those soldiers had known followers of Christ that had directly known some of Jesus' disciples? It's not impossible, chronologically, and imagining the possibility made it all the more fascinating.

For the person who doesn't appreciate history but enjoys modern fantasy, George R.R. Martin, who wrote *Game of Thrones*, was inspired by Hadrian's Wall on a visit to England once, where he imagined himself as a Roman legionary standing at the wall looking north into vast fields, curious as to which savages they would encounter if they moved beyond. In fact, Hadrian's Wall was the inspiration for "The Wall" that kept out the wildlings and White Walkers to the north in *Game of Thrones*.

As an ancient history student who usually reads books and doesn't google pictures online, I hadn't actually seen a real image of what Hadrian's Wall looks like today. I pictured something half the size of the Great Wall of China in height and width. We could not find it using the GPS, so we drove slightly off the road through a long dirt driveway into a farmer's field to ask for directions.

This farmer and his wife had a lovely stone house nestled on some hilly green land with a variety of cows and sheep. This guy was the real live version of the farmer in the *Shaun the Sheep* stop motion animation series. He wore some tall rubber boots and I could imagine that they were just about to go inside their warm stone house to eat a dinner of bangers and mash. He was incredibly kind and polite, and directed us down the road, assuring us that we weren't very far. According to this farmer, with just a quick 10-minute drive we would be there. The sun was still out, but it was fading quickly. We were cutting it close.

As we were leaving the long driveway, one of the farmer's cows was now standing on the dirt path, blocking our car's exit. It was one of the more unfortunate delays: the cow was in our way, the farmer went back into his house, and Ben wouldn't honk the car horn because he didn't want to startle the thing. Ben chose a more conservative attempt at getting the cow to move and flashed his car headlights. The cow turned but didn't budge from the road. So, Ben flashed it again with the high beams. This time, though - the flash lit up the back of the cow where we could see its behind, covered in blood and other fleshy parts dangling from the back. The quick illumination of the high beams etched that image into my memory. I'm not sure if the cow was giving birth or had just done so, but I had seen enough and I didn't want to investigate any further.

With great reluctance, the animal slowly stepped off the path and we were able to get on our way. We were free at last! All that excitement wore on my patience and my bladder though, and I now had to pee. After narrowly escaping the carnage of the bovine's dangling uterus, I didn't want to turn back. Eager to get out of there we pressed on the gas and drove for a few minutes until I asked Ben to pull over. I felt bad for further delaying our trip since the sun was almost down and we really wanted a picture of that wall.

Since I didn't want anyone to see me pee, I wandered away from the road and found a pile of rocks that were out of sight from oncoming traffic. Relief filled my body as I released the jitters and urine that had been building up since we left the airport. As I did my business, I couldn't help but stand in awe of the view. The emerald green hills and golden sunset were stunning. To be honest, it was probably the most captivating pee I ever took.

Ben figured he would take advantage of this bathroom break too, so he walked further down from where I was standing so I couldn't see him (I was thankful for this since I had already seen enough disturbing imagery that day). Before getting back on the road, Ben suggested that he read a sign that was a few feet away from him. As I was walking back to the car, I heard Ben shout with great excitement (and confusion), "Dallas! This is Hadrian's Wall - we are here, and I think we just peed on it!"

I ran back to where I had just relieved myself and sure enough, what I thought was a pile of rocks, was a strip of small stone hedges. There wasn't much left of the wall, and what was left was only a couple of feet off the ground as it was mostly in ruins. I could still see the steam from my urine coming off of it. I tried to reconcile the magnificent Wall I imagined in my mind, with the pile of pee coated rubble I saw before me. The whole thing was a letdown.

Two years after our trip, *Game of Thrones* would debut on television. One of the main characters in the *Game of Thrones* show, Tyrion Lannister, famously says of "The Wall", "I just want to stand on top of the Wall and piss off the edge of the world." Tyrion's statement makes me wonder, was George R.R. Martin on the same trip as us? Did he see us peeing that evening? And if so, does that mean I'm entitled to some *Game of Thrones* royalties?

THE PASTOR'S PORRIDGE
~ For Edwin Wiebe ~

My house is at war with the humidity that Ontario relentlessly seems to bring each year. Productivity goes down, tempers flare, and fuses shorten for all in our house. It was 8:30 am and it felt like 35 degrees Celsius without the humidity. My father, who is part man, part machine, was over the previous night installing the electric wiring that was needed for the recent purchase of our ductless air conditioner. They could not arrive soon enough from Quebec, where I ordered them from. The units themselves take a couple of days to install, and we'd be installing it on one of the hottest summers on record.

I finished my morning coffee and was now ready to begin the day of helping my father complete the installation and bring some relief to our house. It would likely take us the entire day in 42 degree Celsius heat to get it all functional. I raised my sweaty leg off the leather recliner with coffee in hand and as I did, I could hear and feel the ripping of my legs from the welding that happened from sitting for 15 minutes. When I looked back, I half expected to see my flesh attached to the couch. Both of my legs were red.

Whenever there is an unbearably hot day, I'm reminded of a story that my grandpa told me many times as a child (Grandpa loves to tell the same stories with the same level of enthusiasm every time). My grandpa, Edwin Wiebe, is one of the best storytellers I've ever met, which is probably why so many of his tales are seared in my memory.

My grandpa's side of the family emigrated from Russia in the late 1800s to Manitoba and Saskatchewan. They were Germans (Mennonites) living on Russian land for almost 100 years. This land was given to them from the Russian Czarina (Catherine) to be cultivated. The Czarina extended an offer to the Mennonites in Germany to work the land in Russia, while allowing them the freedom to practice Christianity. The Mennonites were able to set up their own schools, stay out of the military, have governance on the land and even continue to speak German with no pressure to learn Russian. The covering for German Mennonites in Russia became threatened when the Bolshevik Revolution was on the horizon and there was mounting pressure for military conscription (which they feared they would be persecuted for rejecting). Canada had been offering free land on the prairies to "hearty European farming peoples" around the same time, and Mennonites and Ukrainians were their first pick to bring over. Canada would also guarantee their religious freedoms and freedom from conscription.

My grandpa's family came from a German tradition that valued living humble lives of hard work and simplicity, while being strongly rooted in their faith, no matter what hardships they encountered. Grandpa would eventually leave the Mennonite church, taking what good he found there, to get more involved with the Baptists, and eventually meandering his way over to the Pentecostal church where he is presently one of the oldest practicing pastors in the denomination.

My grandpa was privy to witnessing some of the 1940s and 50s "big tent revival meetings" as a young man. These tent revivals left a big impact on him. He experienced God in a tangible way that really impacted his faith, and he's been a committed man ever since. When my grandpa tells a story, it is slowed down and delivered with great intention and care. When he prays, it's the same way. "Thoughts and prayers" has become a bit of a meaningless phrase nowadays, but when Grandpa says he will pray for you, he means it. If you are sick, tired, stressed, he will go to war for you in the way that any good Mennonite would - through prayer, fasting and a generous offering of practical support.

Grandpa felt a call to pastor, preach and teach from a very young age. He's never been wealthy in the material sense of the word, and as long as I've known him, he's worn the same simple clothing and read scripture every day. Back when he was a little younger, he accompanied a few other pastors on a trip to India to do some open-air tent revival meetings.

He didn't know much about India before he went. He arrived at the airport in his dress shirt and dress pants, probably the same ones he wears today, to be honest. I used to joke with him when I was younger about how he always wears the same clothes, but as I get older I see the appeal and find myself wearing a lot of the same outfits too. It's just way easier. In fact, as a long time Star Trek fan, one of the things I admire beyond all their scientific and technological advances, is the fact that everyone on the show wears simple "onesies." I hope human civilization moves in that direction someday.

When he landed in India, Grandpa took one step out of the airplane and was immediately drenched in his own sweat, hit by a wall of humid air mass that wouldn't go away until he flew back to Canada. He was put up in a hotel with the rest of his team and was given a few days to recover from jet lag before they would begin their meetings. The hotel they stayed in had no air conditioning. What it did have were half rusted black ceiling fans dotted throughout the building to provide some sense of relief.

After a night's sleep, my grandpa made his way to the room where they held a breakfast buffet. He was quite hungry from what was basically 24 hours of travel after layovers and stops were factored in, and his biological clock was off course.

As he made his way towards the table, a waiter looked at his nametag and said, "Mr. Wiebe, please do not drink the tap water. Only drink the bottled water on the tables." My grandpa assumed that the tap water was the only item he would have to be wary of. He later found out that this assumption was very wrong indeed.

There were many breakfast items that Grandpa wasn't familiar with, and not wanting to be too risky with the choices, he opted for some toast, fruit and raisin porridge. He ate his breakfast, joined the rest of the team, and set out to do their first meeting. They continued this schedule for the next several days before most of the team became quite ill (Grandpa included), ironic because they came to pray for the sick and offer financial support for the poor, something he's done faithfully for his entire life.

Grandpa had been sick for a few days and as he gradually began to feel better, made his way down to the breakfast buffet because he had only been able to keep water and porridge down. He felt that he needed more nourishment than just the porridge.

He grabbed his bottle of water off the table, nodding to the waiter as he passed by, and reached for a bowl to fill up with porridge. Not eating much besides the oatmeal in the last few days, he thought he'd add some toast and fruit to his plate too. However, as he slowly stepped over to the giant silver vat that warmed the porridge, he reached out with the ladle to get his first scoop. As he was scooping, he noticed a raisin fall from the ceiling, right into the porridge vat. He put the ladle down, took a step back and looked up, where he could see the old black fans running fast and then slower with intermittent power cuts.

He looked back to his bowl, the same bowl of porridge he had been eating all week. He picked one of the raisins out of his bowl thinking, "Well, maybe this is how they put raisins in their porridge here." As he analyzed the little black raisin between his index finger and thumb he noticed it had wings, and so did the other raisins in his bowl. Flies had been dropping from the fans above onto the food below, and he hadn't even noticed.

Grandpa wasn't too phased by his inadvertent insect eating. He pushed through his sickness, stomached those flies (not before praying over his food first) and carried on with the open-air meetings like a champion.

The image of Grandpa naively eating flies is one that is seared in my brain. That experience in India didn't scar my grandpa though. In fact, one of his favourite dishes to this day is his famous rice pudding porridge with raisins that he offers me whenever I visit him. I found out later that while he was eating flies each morning in India, he was singing the old hymn, "I'll Fly Away" each evening as part of the tent services. I know my Grandpa has a great sense of humour, but in this case, I think the good Lord does too.

Ice Aged

~ For Aaron D. ~

Back in 2010, we lived in Burlington, Ontario on the second floor of a small apartment that had light brown parquet flooring. The floor gave off a shine from the thick wax that our landlord used to polish it with. The surface was deceptive though because even though it looked shiny and clean, the variation of colour in the wood made it difficult to tell how filthy the floor actually was. This deception resulted in my wife and I going long stretches of time before we'd finally decide to give it a good washing.

One cold evening in December, I sat in my living room on my ugly tartan couch, watching a TV show I wasn't particularly enjoying. It was one of those evenings where I was watching TV while introspectively wondering what I was doing with my life. I sat there experiencing a mixture of guilt, tiredness and apathy. Hannah was out visiting some girl friends for the weekend so it was just me, my TV, my ugly couch and aquarium; it was the perfect weekend for an introvert like myself.

I sat there aimlessly flipping through channels, scanning the room's surroundings. My naturally planted aquarium sat off to the right and lit up the room with a green glow, a result of the white artificial LED lights that reflected the vegetation in the tank. Next to the tank was my tall IKEA bookshelf (made of that cheap beige chipboard) that contained way too many of my books. With the TV in my periphery, I gathered that perhaps it would be a good night to give the floor a long overdue cleaning. Even though I had no idea whether the floor was dirty or not, I figured it could earn me some brownie points later on with my wife.

The temperature was a bitter -40 degrees Celsius with the windchill that evening, which was unusual for southern Ontario in the winter. And while it was cold outside, I figured it would be a good night to mop since our apartment felt like it was +40 degrees inside. If I mopped the floor, it would likely dry quickly and I'd reduce the risk of slipping and breaking my bones, something I had almost done the last time I undertook this task (and more likely, the real reason why I had neglected mopping for so long).

I kept a meaningless television sitcom running in the background because it made me feel like I wasn't completely alone. I grabbed a large blue bucket from the pantry, filled it up with hot water from the tub and poured some vinegar in before grabbing my mop and getting to work. When I was growing up, my mom used vinegar and hot water to clean things, and now as an adult, I don't use store bought solutions because it just doesn't feel clean if it doesn't have that vinegar smell lingering in the air.

I'm not sure what it is, but I have a compulsion in me when I mop that compels me to avoid touching the wet floor at all costs. I planned my mopping specifically so I could begin at one end of the house and make my way back to the living room. From there, I could leap from the last remaining dry spot on the floor and onto the couch where I could remain until the surface dried. Just before I made my final plunge, I opened the sliding balcony door and placed the mop and bucket of water outside. Once the floor was dry, my plan was to bring the items inside to dispose of the mop water as per the usual process.

However, about five minutes after my successful moping mission, my cell phone rang. Thankfully, the phone was on the couch and not somewhere in the living room that would require me to play "the floor is lava" in order to find it. I picked up my phone, and it was my brother. He had called to tell me about this awesome new show called *The Walking Dead*. He and I have very similar tastes in TV shows, and as I listened to him describe it, he had me instantly sold on it.

I hung up the phone and immediately found the pilot episode online. I love apocalyptic stories about survival, grit and problem-solving. The show is about a large cast of people from diverse backgrounds that are trying to evade the spread of a zombie virus that begins to overwhelm society. They try to stay alive under the near-constant threat of attacks from zombies, nicknamed "walkers." However, it overtakes society and structures of government and stability quickly erode, resulting in an increase in tribalism. Knowing who to trust becomes incredibly precious and risky. As the episodes progress, the zombies aren't nearly as scary as the humans who attempt to survive one another. Plus, the main character has a cowboy hat (the same kind I wear all summer) and is guided by a strong moral compass. It's kind of like watching an adult version of Woody from *Toy Story*.

Before I knew it, I had watched four episodes straight. I figured I needed to sleep but was too scared to make my way down the dark hallway to my bedroom, so I dozed off on the couch. The next day, I woke up and walked to the kitchen on my freshly cleaned floors to make my morning coffee. With my mug in hand, I went over to the balcony window to stare at the snow while drinking my morning brew.

As I took another sip, I noticed that I had forgotten to bring the mop and bucket of dirty water into the house from the previous night. Since it was so cold out, the water was now ice and had assumed the shape of the bucket. With the bitter cold air, there was no way the water would thaw outside. I wondered how I would troubleshoot the new issue of getting the frozen mop water out of the bucket. I was only a sip or two into my morning coffee as my mind began to explore my options. I thought about dumping the giant ice cube in the shared garbage bin, but then realized it would just leak everywhere once it melted. I then considered bringing the bucket-shaped block into my house to let it melt in my tub, but it would take all day for the ice to melt.

The best course of action I could think of was to tip the bucket over, allow the ice to slide out and throw the large block over the balcony into the area below. The yard wasn't really one specific person's backyard, it was a large, shared area where the tenants below had sliding glass doors that walked out into the space. The ice would be in the shape of a bucket, but eventually, it would warm up and melt. I began to have doubts about my plan though and wondered, *What if my aim is off and I end up smashing someone's lawn ornaments, or worse yet, their glass deck?* As I took my last sip, I solved my quandary.

I settled on flipping the bucket upside down and allowing the large ice cube to slide out onto my concrete balcony floor. There, I'd chip away at it with a hammer until the chunks became small enough that I could simply sweep them over the balcony ledge below where it wouldn't cause damage. So, that's what I decided on. Except, when I flipped the bucket over and the ice cube slid out, I let out a startled yelp because inside the ice staring back at me was a dead squirrel. At first, I couldn't tell if it was dead or alive because its eyes looked like they were open and staring at me. And then, I wondered if it was possible for it to survive a deep freeze of twelve hours. *Surely, according to science, this squirrel is officially dead with no hope of unthawing itself back to life?* I mulled that statement over in my head several times until I believed it.

How the heck did this even happen, I wondered? The only dots I could connect were that our back yard had a lot of trees where squirrels were often found scurrying around. The night prior, one must have jumped from the tree onto our balcony thinking there was food and became trapped in the bucket of warm vinegar water, unable to escape. I would have heard it if I hadn't had the TV on so loud.

My original plan was useless now. If I broke the cube down with a hammer, then I'd also have to sweep the dead squirrel into my neighbours' patio area below. If I let the cube thaw in my tub, it would be filled with dead rodent bacteria, the same problem I'd have if I disposed of it in our communal garbage area. Plus, it would end up really smelling bad, and would surely break some building hygiene rules.

I didn't know what to do. If I threw the entire cubed carcass over the balcony, somebody would see me. If it wasn't someone in my own complex, it could be any of the homeowners directly across from us (they were close enough that they could see what I was doing if their blinds were open, as they often were).

In the end, I decided to leave the ice encompassed critter on my balcony until the sun went down, when I could then go back outside and launch the entire thing off the ledge as far as I could, hoping it wouldn't land in my neighbour's yard. And, with the moonlight,

I'd be able to ensure that I didn't accidentally hit someone in the head with it, bonus.

And so, like a criminal in the night, I waited till the darkness set in, shut all the lights off in my apartment and awkwardly heaved the hunk of ice like an Olympian shot-putter. I breathed a sigh of relief as I heard it hit the snow below. After my successful mission, I went inside as if nothing had ever happened and turned on the TV to watch some more of my new favourite show. Thankfully, my wife wasn't there for all of this. She might have called the police on me herself or had them assess my mental capacity for being able to be left on my own.

The following day, I woke up (again, on the couch due to fear from the zombies) and I headed back to the kitchen to grab my coffee. I poured my cup and walked over to the living room to feed my fish. As I was looking at my aquarium and taking slow slips of my hot beverage, I could hear children playing outside in the distance (there is something so precious about the sound of children laughing and having fun). I made my way over to my balcony window; the wind had died down from the day before and it was a calm, sunny winter day. The freshly fallen snow on the pine trees glistened in the sunlight, it looked so peaceful outside.

I was trying to look past the children to see where the squirrel had landed, but couldn't see it. As I looked closer, I noticed that the kids had built a tall snow fort in the backyard. To my shock, atop their fort was the ice encompassed squirrel, with its fluffy tail dangling out. One kid was petting the tail with his winter gloves, like a crazy person. *What is wrong with kids these days?* I wondered. For a brief moment, I debated going outside to save the children (or was it the squirrel who needed saving?) but then I reasoned, *Who am I to ruin their fun winter day?* I decided to leave the kids alone and slowly backed into my house from the balcony, shut the door, closed the windows and hoped that I wouldn't be implicated in some sort of "cruelty to animals" crime I wasn't aware of.

I learned a valuable lesson that weekend. Next time, my wife can wash the floors.

WHEN LIFE GIVES YOU LEMSIP
~ For David S. ~

It was summertime. I had just finished a B.A. in History. In 2009, I set my mind towards completing my degree after confidently asserting in my heart for several years that University wasn't for me. It took three years to complete the degree while my wife worked a job she didn't enjoy in order to pay the bills while I was at school most days. We tag-teamed it in the hope that by obtaining my degree, it would make life easier for us and our family down the road.

I was so focused on completing my degree that I hadn't given much thought towards what to do after it was finished. My thinking was that those sorts of problems would sort themselves out when the time came. The irony was that I had spent the last three years trying to think critically and analytically towards a variety of topics to demonstrate competency and coherence of thought, meanwhile, I hadn't even reflected upon how this degree would help me pay the bills.

Well, the time had come. I had handed in my final assignment, a large research paper on the role of religion in the Vietnam War. I received an A as my final mark, in my final class, which meant my degree was officially over. I felt accomplished, knowing I'd finished my program, which was followed by immediate dread and anxiety about not knowing what I was going to do next.

I went to the local temp agency to look for work. I applied to anything that wasn't hard manual labour. Two weeks passed, and I heard nothing. I told myself it was a honeymoon period and that I'd get something soon. Four weeks passed, and by this time I had handed out numerous resumes and cover letters to a variety of employment options that had absolutely no requirement for a B.A. in History.

I felt a little depressed, highly anxious, and regretted not having put more thought into a long term goal for the last three years. The anxiety got out of hand, and it ended up being one of the worst summers of my life because I could not unhook my racing mind from all of the uncertainties.

I went to bed one night and noticed my phone had a missed voicemail in the morning. It was a call from the temp agency stating they found a position for me at a pharmaceutical company. I could start work the following week if I wanted the job - my opportunity had come at last! According to the temp agency, the job offered competitive pay, had room for growth and if the company liked me, it could turn into a full-time salaried position with benefits. The job had nothing to do with what I studied at University, but it sounded better than anything else I could find. Eagerly, I accepted the role.

I was told very little about the job other than the fact that I would need to wear a white lab coat, do some health and safety training and show up with steel-toed work shoes. The rest of the details would be given to me on my first day of work.

My mind started racing as I imagined what the role could look like and I couldn't help but get excited about the prospects ahead. Based on my Resume, I suspected that they hired me for some sort of research or administrative work. This made me slightly nervous since I had no background in chemistry or biology (which I imagined was required in someone who works for a pharmaceutical company). I envisioned myself walking around a laboratory wearing a white coat, carrying beakers with dangerous chemicals and analyzing data through plastic safety glasses.

They told me the lab ran 24 hours a day in shifts, and I'd start my day at 12pm and finish at 8 pm. The middle shift. This made sense since I figured this lab was doing important "pharmaceutical work" that required consistent round the clock output. Looking back, this was a funny thought since I had no clue what "pharmaceutical work" entailed.

The following week came, and I felt a great sense of purpose as I hopped in my car to drive to my first day of work. Even though I knew I'd be wearing a lab coat, I chose to wear dress pants and a dress shirt with my best tie. *Dress for the job you want, not the one you have*, I thought to myself.

The GPS led me to a bland brick building in an industrial area of the city. I parked my car and walked towards the entrance. I rang the buzzer to a darkened glass door that didn't look very inviting. A lady opened the door slightly and spoke with an annoyed tone through the gap, "Are you a new hire?" she squawked, "New hires have to enter through the warehouse door."

I walked over to the warehouse side of the building where I saw several people in white lab coats sitting off to the side at a worn-down picnic table. There were hundreds of cigarette butts littered on the ground. Two ladies sat there, smoking, in silence. They scanned me up and down, with a disappointed look on their faces. They reminded me of Patty and Selma from *The Simpsons* both in their looks and raspiness of voice. I smiled at them and walked towards the door entrance and pushed the buzzer. A man, who happened to be the manager, opened the door and I enthusiastically told him that I was the new hire, ready to start for today's 12pm shift. He led me down a hallway into a small conference room that was already filled with seven other new hires who didn't look as excited about being there. That's when the tide of optimism began to turn for me.

The manager did a very brief five minute presentation on the company vision and purpose but hadn't actually outlined what our jobs would entail. He was like the manager, Michael Scott from *The Office* TV show, over-exaggerating the significance of the job we were hired to do, but without any of the humour. He talked at length about how he was able to cut costs and save money for the company, and he seemed very proud of this. You could tell that people in the room just wanted him to get to the point, and explain what our roles would look like.

He stated that we were handpicked by the temp agency for our skills and experience and that we would be helping provide medicinal products to the community to ease pain and suffering. It was obvious by the tone in his voice that even he didn't believe what he was saying. He sounded scripted and mechanical, just like the machines I was about to be put to work on. He let us know that while our contracts were only for a probationary three month period, if we showed promise and skill, there was a good possibility of being hired into a full-time capacity.

I thought, *Ok, I can hack working for low pay for three months if it leads to something much better.* While the manager was giving us his orientation, he made a comment about how his son was just finishing University and was travelling around Europe "wasting his time and getting it out of his system" before he'd have to come back to Canada and take up a boring job like his old man, because "that's what real life is like." He laughed as he said this. He seemed well-meaning in trying to convey that he knew what the real world was like and that his son lived in a fairytale land of naivety and needed to be realistic about what to expect regarding work and life. I sat there thinking, *What a short outlook on life, education, and employment. What if your kid decides to stay in Europe or finds a job that he finds meaning and joy doing?* I understand that a variety of circumstances can lead many people to employment they might not want to do, through little choice of their own, but that's not always the case. I could tell from his outlook, that I was about to walk into something I wouldn't be excited about.

We were told to leave our belongings in a locker and were led down another hallway to a much larger room with an industrial sized lab that was fitted with loud fans, ventilation and machinery. The manager said, "Welcome to Room A, this is where you will be working. Your job will be to package packets of lemon cold and flu mix into their appropriate boxes, which will then be mailed to stores across Canada and the US providing relief to hundreds of thousands of people.

You'll learn how the process and machinery work here, and you will be guided by the floor supervisor who will inspect the process each night to ensure a smooth running operation."

My heart sank; this wasn't a lab; this was a factory for lemon flavoured cold medicine. In front of me was a large machine that took up the entire length of the room. Six workers stood along the side of the machine, each holding a different position on the line to ensure the process ran smoothly. One man was the machine mechanic, he stood on a ladder manning the top where the machine's engine was, ensuring a speedy correction in case there were any malfunctions. Just below him was another guy whose sole job was to run bags of sugar over to another ladder to be poured into a giant holding tank and dispenser that sat within the machine.

The machine would then mix 85% sugar content with acetaminophen and lemon flavouring into small packets which would spit out onto a conveyor belt. The mechanic could often be heard ranting about how disgusting the flu and cold packets were and he said on numerous occasions that it would be far healthier to eat an actual lemon with some honey than drinking this concoction. In the words of the mechanic, "It goes against my conscience to be the one enabling the creation of this stuff, but hey, I've got bills to pay."

There was also one person whose job was to wipe the conveyor belt with a rag periodically, and another whose role was to sweep the floors to ensure no sugar accumulating. The supervisor had the best job - he would just stand around watching what everyone else was doing.

The conveyor belt dumped the flu and cold packets out like tire tubes on a lazy river, which would sail down the line to two other workers who assembled cardboard cartons that would be boxed and ready for shipment. The pattern was: turn the machine on, ensure it doesn't stall, pour sugar and active ingredients into the machine, scoop up 12 packets off the line, throw them into a box, close the box, toss it to the side for someone else to pick and stack on skids for shipping to another part of the warehouse. I was given the role of scooping the packets up and putting them in the boxes. You did this same pattern for every seven hour shift. This was not at all the "pharmaceutical work" I imagined.

The "lab" where this operation happened had chemical white walls, hospital blue laminate flooring, which made sweeping spilled sugar easy, and blinding white fluorescent lights in the ceiling that hummed aggressively.

The job was monotonous, repetitive, and lacked any need for creativity. I was bored after the first shift and couldn't see myself thriving there. I tried to imagine myself pushing past the three month mark and earning a more livable salary doing this. Any scenario where I contemplated this, made me feel despair and hopelessness. I felt stuck but figured I shouldn't quit and I should give it a good shot since it had been so hard to find a job.

Beyond the monotony, the worst part of this job was the

environment. I went outside to text my wife on one of my "lunch" breaks, where some employees were outside smoking. One of them, (Patty or Selma), said, "Hey, new guy, you don't have to show off in there." I had no idea what she was talking about. Her friend then quipped, "Yeah, you don't have to wear a tie, it won't earn you any more money." I didn't know what to say, so I said, "I'm sorry, it's my first day and I wanted to put my best foot forward."

I explained to them that after graduating from University, I found this role through a temp agency and I was eager to learn and grow. I never should have disclosed that though, because from that point on, they nagged me at every moment they could, even while we were working the assembly line. They'd say things like, "A lot of good that piece of paper and school debt did you, only to land you here" always followed by a maniacal laugh with intermittent wheezing. Determined to get through my probationary period, I resolved to not let Patty and Selma get to me.

And, just in case I still had any hope, Selma, who had been there for years and took the coveted "sweeper" job, took me aside on my third night to tell me not to go getting any ideas about trying to get hired full time, since there was a growing list of temp employees who were higher up on the seniority list. A supervisor, who was younger than me on the shift told all of us on our break that if we worked hard, we could one day possibly be promoted to a supervisor role like he was doing. He had been doing this job right out of high school and was only the supervisor for the overnight shift because nobody wanted to do it since it really wears on your body. For each night I was there, I'd see him drinking a can of Red Bull. His skin looked incredibly pale and like he needed a serious amount of sleep.

On my fifth night there, our first break was about to begin and I got off my stool where I sat and grabbed a broom to sweep up a little sugar near my feet where one of the packets had leaked. Selma came back and noticed me sweeping. Like an angry police officer, she barked, "Hey, are you trying to steal my job?" Her job was to sweep spilled sugar and cleaning up after my own mess really upset her. At this point, I knew it was time for me to go. I didn't want to work in an environment where I'd be ridiculed and step on everyone's toes. While I had no other job prospects lined up, the anxiety I had about finding employment that summer paled in comparison to the drudgery I felt when I thought about working at "Lemsip".

Having the courage to walk away from a job isn't always risky for someone in their 20's who has nothing to lose. Patty and Selma likely didn't have that same privilege though, which is sometimes the tragic reality of the system we work within. For my own well-being, I needed to walk away. That evening, I went to the manager's office (who wasn't there during the night shift) dropped my assigned door key on his desk, returned the plastic protective glasses and lab coat I was issued, and walked to my car and drove home: I had quit. The drive home was so liberating.

A few days later, I received an email from another employment recruiter who was looking for someone to teach English in Korea. I had no plan or training for this role, and this opportunity presented itself out of nowhere. In fact, it seemed way too wild of an idea to actually consider.

After some back and forth communication with the recruiter and negotiating with my wife's employer, we boarded a plane to Korea where I found a job teaching English that took me way out of my comfort zone and put me on a completely different trajectory than the one the pharmaceutical manager had painted for me.

It turns out that "the real world" doesn't just have to be the little bit of travelling you get out of your system before you have to return to a job that makes you resentful. I hope that the manager's son came to the same realization.

When life gives you Lemsip, sometimes you're better off catching the travel bug.

SISTER KIM'S KIMCHI
~ For Tamara & Duane ~

I used to love flying until a flight home from London, England had some pretty rough turbulence coming into Toronto. The plane felt like it was violently jerking from left to right for a few terrifying moments. I gripped the seat, unsettled, colour draining from my face. I had never felt something like that on a plane before and never want to again. Ever since that flight, I've preferred the train.

A couple of years later, I took a job teaching English in Korea. It would require flying from Toronto to New York, and then New York directly to Seoul, a sixteen-and-a-half-hour flight. When I heard how long I'd be in the air, I almost turned down the job due to fear of having to fly for that long.

The embarrassment of turning down a once in a lifetime job opportunity overpowered my fear, however, and I decided to board that Asiana Airlines flight. I'm glad I did because it was one of the smoothest flights I've ever been on, and the Korean flight attendants, food and service were like nothing I've experienced on a Canadian airline.

One of my biggest fears was that the plane could crash in open water if the engines gave out and nobody would be able to find us. Even if the plane managed to crash land in the water successfully, I always imagined myself hanging onto some piece of luggage with my legs dangling in the water like Jack did when Kate was floating on that wooden door in the movie, *Titanic*. Needless to say, flying

28

over water makes me more nervous than land.

I knew that the Pacific Ocean stood between Canada and Korea and flying over it for a significant portion of our time in the air made me unsettled. I was pleasantly surprised when I learned that I was looking at the journey from the perspective of a world map that didn't reflect aviation scale accurately. The fastest way to Korea from the East Coast of North America is actually to fly up to the Arctic Circle (almost to the North Pole) and then come back down through Russia and China, and then finally into Korea.

When I'm flying, one of the things I do to ease my anxiety is watch the flight tracker on the mini screen on the back of the seat. I follow the little airplane icon as it makes its way to the final destination. Once the plane icon completes a pass over a body of water, my anxiety goes down. In this case, I really just had to wait it out as it flew over Hudson's Bay and up to the Arctic Ocean. The Arctic Ocean is mostly ice, so it didn't count as a real ocean, I rationalized. Thankfully, our flight path completely avoided the Pacific Ocean, which made the trip a little more bearable for me.

About an hour and a half before landing, the pilot came onto the microphone and stated that the flight would have to make a slight detour due to "North Korean activity." I scanned the reactions of the passengers around me; most of the people on the flight were Korean and appeared unmoved by this announcement. I immediately went into panic mode though as I imagined the plane getting knocked out of the sky by missile launches. I prayed in my seat, *God, why would you allow me to have such a great flight here, avoid the entire Pacific Ocean and in the fifteenth hour, let a rocket blow us up?*

I'd find out later at Incheon International Airport, that North Korea did indeed launch a rocket but it was a successful satellite launch into orbit and not intercontinental ballistic missiles, which is what they are usually threatening the United States with. North Korea has done quite a few missile practice launches in the past where they have not had much control over the trajectory of their own rockets, so I feel that my apprehension was valid.

Prior to boarding my flight, I was told I would be picked up at the airport by a man called Mr. Shim who would drive me to my hotel, and that's all I knew. Mr. Shim was waiting in the arrivals area and greeted me with a smile as he took my suitcase and motioned to follow him quickly to his car outside. Mr. Shim didn't speak any English, so our one and a half-hour car ride to my hotel was spent in silence.

My hotel was actually something Koreans call a "love motel" and it was meant for couples to rent on an hourly basis to show their affection for one another. I didn't know this when I stayed there though. It did, however, explain why my bed was shaped like a heart. The school had arranged this hotel for me prior to my flight and they did so because it's quite cheap to stay there compared to other upscale hotels. Mr. Shim walked me up to my room on the third floor. I opened the door and walked in. He started to yell at me, pointing at my shoes, making hand signals telling me to take them off. Apparently, it's disrespectful to enter a room with your shoes on. I took my shoes off and he threw me a pair of slippers, then he bowed his head and left me on my own with no further instructions about who or when someone would contact me next. I did not care though, I was jet lagged beyond belief and just wanted to sleep.

I hadn't eaten in five hours and remembered that I saw a large vending machine in the lobby of the motel entrance. I had some cash and figured I could get something to eat to hold me over for the night until I could venture out in the morning for real food. While I wasn't too familiar with Korean culture, I knew that Korea had a reputation for having fantastic food so I wasn't too worried about finding any.

I went down to the lobby, only to find a vending machine filled to the brim with phallic paraphernalia. That was no help to me, even though some of the items had an "edible" symbol on them. I wasn't that desperate for food so I went to bed hungry. The jetlag was so bad, I slept through the night and into most of the following day, waking up at 6 pm local time. I rushed out the door and onto the street, hoping I could get some food before any restaurants might close. The area my motel was in seemed a little bit shady; there were a number of shops and restaurants around me but the area around my motel appeared quiet and eerie since there weren't many people around. It amplified my feelings of being alone and isolated.

One thing that stood out to me was some large rectangular aquariums filled with live squid and octopus that sat outside a restaurant. This restaurant looked vacant, but I could see an old lady sitting at one of the tables, presumably the owner. I figured that maybe times were hard and she could use my business. Or maybe this was just a sparsely populated area and that's why no one was there? I decided to go in, because *When has an old Korean lady ever not made good food?* I reasoned. I was excited to eat, but slightly nervous because I wasn't one to venture very far outside of my culinary comfort zone. I knew that Koreans were big into their kimchi and rice, but that was the extent of my food knowledge. I really should have learned more about Korea before deciding to live there.

I opened the door and proceeded to walk to an empty table. The lady yelled at me to take my shoes off (I had already forgotten about that rule), and I made my way to a table on the floor where I sat down cross-legged. Sitting down on the floor to eat really made me feel like I was in Asia. The lady in the restaurant spoke no English and there was no menu with pictures either, so the only way I could order food was by pointing to my stomach and shrugging. The Korean lady just nodded and walked back to her stainless-steel kitchen and started cooking. I was the only one in the tiny restaurant of five tables. There was a Samsung flatscreen TV on the wall, but it wasn't on.

Ten minutes later, she brought out a tray with a sizzling stone bowl of rice, veggies, beef and kimchi as well as six small metal side dishes with fermented radish, peanuts, beansprouts and more kimchi. The presentation took up the entire table, and she watched me take my first few bites from her kitchen window with a smile on her face.

In Korea, they put red chili peppers in everything. Growing up on the standard prairie palette of mashed potatoes, gravy and roast beef, I had no palette for spicy food whatsoever. I didn't want to offend her by not being able to finish the food, but it felt like hellfire was purifying my body and soul with every bite I took. My face was sweating, and my nose was running like a hose.

She then walked over to my table and pulled out a book and began speaking words I couldn't understand while handing me literature I couldn't read. She then turned on the large Samsung TV and began to play a religious DVD of some sort. It was a Korean man delivering a sermon as fiery as her homemade kimchi. Within a few moments, we both had tears streaming down our face, but for different reasons.

She stood to the side of the flatscreen and closed her eyes while praying loudly, tears passionately running down her face. I sat there in shock trying to finish my food, wondering, *What the heck is happening here? Did I offend her because I can't finish my meal? Was she upset because I didn't take off my shoes?* Thoughts raced through my mind as I tried to assess what was happening while wiping snot from my runny nose.

I knew Korea had a lot of Christians, so I figured she was trying to share her faith with me but I wasn't too sure because something seemed "off." I tried telling her that I was already a Christian but she just ignored me. She grabbed my hands and prayed. I bowed my head and prayed too. *What harm could there be in praying with her?* I thought. So, I prayed a prayer of blessing over her and her business in English and thanked her for her bizarre service.

As I paid for the meal, she handed me a piece of paper to sign, which I did, thinking it was a receipt of some sort. I put my shoes on real fast and ran out of there like Sonic the Hedgehog. I sprinted back to the hotel with my mind full of questions and my face still on fire. I tried running with my mouth open so the breeze could cool my lips. I probably looked deranged jogging through the street, kind of like those dogs who hang their heads out the car window with their tongues flapping in the wind. Later that night, my phone rang and it was one of the English teachers I'd be working with. He called to let me know I'd be leaving the love motel the next day because my apartment was ready. I was so relieved.

When I recounted my experience to my fellow English teacher, he laughed. He then explained that the lady at the restaurant was a follower of a newly formed cult. The reason there was nobody in the restaurant was because she was trying to convert the patrons, something she'd done to several unsuspecting English teachers in the past as well as local Koreans (who usually got angry with her or shrugged her off). Apparently, by signing that piece of paper I was agreeing to join her cult. Adding my name and others to her list was proof to show her religious leaders that she was increasing the membership. Not a very effective evangelistic technique, but I admired her boldness.

The pamphlets she gave to me were introductions to her cult's teachings, meeting locations and times of their gatherings. Here I was innocently thinking she was just a passionate Christian lady shamelessly inviting me to accept Jesus into my life after having her kimchi (which honestly, was so peppery it could probably absolve sins).

That was my crash course entry into Korea, after being there for only forty-eight hours. As bizarre as it was, I'd prefer to relive that whole experience again than having to fly for sixteen hours.

THE LAND OF THE MORNING WOOD
~ For Gordie ~

Korea is referred to as "The Land of the Morning Calm," a term well suited due to its natural beauty of stunning mountains, clear waters, and splendid peacefulness – particularly in the morning. One of the best ways to experience this calm is to climb to the top of a mountain and observe the surroundings in the early hours of the day. I love climbing mountains because they make me feel small and give me perspective (literally and spiritually). If you've ever reached the top of a mountain after a hard climb, you'll know that all the distractions and worries of life are drowned out by the awe of the view in front of you. Whenever I reach the peak, I'm reminded of what matters most to me: my faith, my family, and my friends.

The tallest mountain I've ever climbed is Mount Seoraksan, the highest mountain in the Taebek range in Northeastern Korea. This mountain overlooks the Sea of Japan to the east and North Korea to the north. Seoraksan means "Snow Rock Mountain," which is literally the case in the fall and winter months. The entire range is magnificent and attracts hikers all throughout the year. There are many different flowers, trees, and steep cliffs of smooth granite that are covered in wisps of mist, making the journey feel mystical.

While Seoraksan is not a treacherous hike, it is a long one. Once you drive to the base of the mountain, it requires another seven hours on foot to reach the top. At the base, there are Siberian pine trees in abundance that cover the lower levels of the range. As you ascend, these coniferous trees gradually turn into oak and other deciduous trees. In the dark, you can actually smell when the foliage changes as the evergreen scent begins to fade away.

The most famous part of the Seoraksan mountain range is the Dinosaur Ridge, which is a stretch of rock that looks like Stegosaurus spikes protruding through the trees and into the sky. We didn't climb the Dinosaur Ridge, since we wanted to climb Daechongbong Peak which, at 5,604 feet is the tallest point of Seoraksan.

My friend Steve and I had planned to hike the mountain throughout the night so that we could reach the peak in time to watch the sunrise over the Sea of Japan. Since most people hike it during the day, we were alone for our nighttime ascent.

Our climb was poorly planned. We had no hiking equipment, no helmets with headlamps, no flashlights, and we only spoke English, while most of the people we met on the mountain were older Koreans that spoke very little English. The trip was a knee jerk decision at the last minute.

All we had were our backpacks, which had some terrible sandwiches and triangle sushi pieces we bought at the local 7-11. As our coach neared the mountain, Steve realized he forgot his water bottle at home. It worked out though because near the foot of the mountain was an old Korean lady in a hut selling food and drinks to hungry hikers. She was selling this brown energy drink in a glass bottle. With nightfall fast approaching, the lady was shutting down shop, so Steve quickly grabbed the last few remaining bottles and threw them in his backpack. The lady gave us a big thumbs up saying, "Good for stamina! Big one!" Perfect, we said. Seven hours uphill all night, some parts quite steep, stamina was exactly what we'd need to get to the top.

We began our climb at twilight, and the moon was only just ascending. We had to squint to see what was ahead of us and then continually re-adjust our eyes as the sun went down. If it had been cloudy, I don't think we could have made the climb. Thankfully, the skies were clear and the mountain range was exposed by the bright white moonlight, giving some insight into where we were walking. Every 20 minutes, we'd take a break to catch our breath and replenish on liquids: water for me, stamina juice for Steve.

At the beginning of the hike, there were waterfalls and natural pools that provided a comforting white noise as we walked. But, as we began to climb higher, the waterfalls disappeared, and with it the noise. For the remaining four hours of the ascent, the climb was in silence - all I could hear was our footsteps, the thoughts in my head and the occasional wind gust.

With no city lights to be seen and no voices to be heard, we became intensely aware of the fact that we were all alone in a national park and out of reach from any help should we need it. It was a very sobering feeling. Around five hours into the hike, we began contemplating whether or not we were lost. We were following what looked like a footpath in the moonlight and assumed that we were on the right track.

The longer we hiked, the more fear began to mount inside of me. In the distance, we could hear a horking and wheezing sound. Curious as to what (or who) we were hearing, we stopped to listen more intently. Around the corner, the bright light on the helmet of an old Korean man shone into our eyes. He was coming down the mountain and had been trying to hork a wad of phlegm trapped in his throat for the better part of 10 minutes. The sounds he was making echoed off the stone in the canyon in a symphony of disgusting melodies. He looked tired, never said hello, but bowed his head as is the custom and went on his way down.

At this point in our hike, Steve's pace began slowing down and he seemed disoriented. Determined to get to the peak, he braced himself as he chugged back his second bottle of stamina juice. It was 4 am and we were exhausted, but we continued on our way.

We were an hour from the top when we heard more grunting sounds and I immediately wondered if bears lived in Korea or if it was another old guy. Up ahead, we could see sleeping bags off to the side of the path, lined up next to one another like a pack of sardines.

As we got closer, I could see that there were bodies in the bags, and they were asleep under the open sky exposed to the elements. The grunting noises we had heard were their snores.

While we were a couple of hours earlier than the sunrise, we had reached the top. Below us, the Sea of Japan glistened in the moonlight and the rest of the mountain range was a cast of dark shadows. A few Korean couples happened to be awake when we arrived, and they invited us to sleep in a little hut near the peak because we didn't have sleeping bags or tents (did I mention how unprepared we were)? We walked into the enclosed hut, which had lights on inside, where about 15 Korean people were sleeping in various positions on the floor. Depleted and dizzy, Steve drank the last of his juice and crumpled into the sea of sleeping Koreans. The nap was well-earned, and we would need all the energy we could get for the next day.

When I woke up a few hours later, I noticed that several of the other hikers were sharing muffled laughs while pointing to someone on the floor. Weary from the hike, it took me a few moments before I clued in to the source of their amusement; they were pointing and laughing at Steve. And as I looked closer, I understood why. Right there in the middle of the floor, beside a few empty juice bottles, Steve's tent was pitched for all to see. The crowd of laughter grew as each waking Korean saw the unsightly sight of both Steve's trash and his testosterone.

I didn't understand why everyone was laughing and I felt embarrassed for my friend. Then, they let me in on the joke. A little Korean lady pointed to the empty beverage containers and explained how Steve had been consuming Beolddeokju –which literally meant, "Erection Wine". Beolddeokju is a rice-based wine containing chestnuts, black and brown sugar – and root extracts like ginseng. The wine is used for men wishing to reach their sexual peak, not that of a mountain. The glass bottle is capped with a porcelain lid in the shape of a penis, something not immediately obvious at first glance. The penile packaging was quite apparent there in the light of the hut but we didn't notice it for the seven hour hike since it was dark out. The wine also had a 13% alcohol content, which explained Steve's difficulties at the top, and why he was currently out-snoring the Koreans.

The rising sun wasn't the only thing we would witness that morning. Steve extended the mountain's tallest peak by a good seven inches, give or take. He was a good sport about it though. After Steve woke up, the other hikers asked if they could pose and take photos with him while they each held a bottle of the empty "Erection Wine".

Steve became a legend on the mountain that day. Thankfully he'd have a good five hours to walk it off on the descent.

NO WAY, JOSÉ!
~ For Melissa ~

A long time ago, I worked in an office with a colleague who was new to Canada, a relatively recent immigrant from Cuba. His name was José. He was short, stocky, bald and always wore stonewashed jeans and a puffy black winter bubble jacket. Despite the office being heated during the winter months, he'd wear the bubble jacket all day with it unzipped, exposing his white t-shirt and silver neck chain. With an upbeat attitude and positive outlook on life, José was an eternal optimist. He was a simple man with a kind heart and poor time management skills. He lived in his own little bubble (in addition to his jacket) which appeared to make sense to him but to no one else.

Our office was open Monday to Friday, but there were numerous times when José showed up to work on Saturday and Sunday, parked his car in the empty lot and made his way to the entrance only to find the front doors locked. I know this because we watched the video camera footage of him attempting to open the front doors, seemingly oblivious to the fact that he was the only person parked in the massive parking lot. I think his body was on autopilot or something, because the footage showed him trying to open the doors, realizing the building was closed, and then happily strutting back to his car to go only God knows where.

José's excitement to get the job done with passion often overshot his ability to do so, but he was great to have in the office for boosting morale. Everybody loved José. His command of the English language was not the greatest but an advantage to this was that you could trust him with your secrets (because chances were he didn't understand them). This backfired on me one day when I told him the day and time for a surprise birthday party we were throwing in the warehouse for a colleague. A little later in the day he went over to that colleague and asked them what time the secret party was starting because he couldn't remember, even though I had just told him an hour earlier. José ruined the surprise, but we couldn't even get mad at him because he was so good-hearted. The best part was when it came time for everyone to meet in the warehouse, José didn't even show up. He sat at his desk working, not noticing that all the employees had trickled out of the office, leaving him behind in his own little world.

In his spare time, José tried to learn English and he often listened to self-help and positive psychology podcasts during his commute to work. In the mornings, he would come into the office and tell us about a new revelation he had received. He'd try to describe what he learned, but it would get lost in translation and we'd all smile and nod like we knew what he was saying, but really, we had no clue.

Back in Cuba, José really liked music and clubbing, but it was hard to make a decent living there so he emigrated to Canada. When he was first hired, José told me that he came to Canada by way of a boat he made out of car parts. I thought he was joking. I'm still not sure if he was pulling my leg or not.

The more I got to know him, the more I realized his story about his dingy made out of car parts could be true. The car he drove to work every day was a real junker, a Picasso of parts and colours from various vehicles. During his breaks, José could be found out in the parking lot, tinkering under the hood. José also had a knack for ingenuity, he was one of those guys who could fix anything using unorthodox means (which made sense when I consider how unorthodox he was, in general). I saw José pick locked doors with paper clips and fix work computers with foil gum wrappers, wire and soldering tools.

For someone who had no sense of time, I discovered that José's bathroom routine ran like clockwork. Every day without fail, he would get up from his cubicle exactly twenty minutes before lunchtime to go relieve himself. José had a unique restroom routine that I'd never seen used by anyone ever before or since. Once he was in the stall, he'd take his shoes and pants off and hang them over the back of the door so he could do his business. As soon as he was half-naked and settled in, José would blare a song on repeat that would play during the entirety of his bathroom stay.

Upon entering the restroom one day, I could hear club music blaring on his speakers. I couldn't make out most of the words except for, "Red light, Green light" which seemed to make up the majority of the song's lyrics. It was a catchy tune and in the reflection of the large sink mirrors I could see José's knees bouncing to the beat. It was quite the scene to stumble upon, and the song was stuck in my head for the rest of the day.

The next morning, José came into the office looking white as a ghost, (his paler shade was made more noticeable when contrasted against his jet black bubble jacket). The cheery glow on his face was gone and he looked shaken up. One headphone was in his ear playing music loud enough for us to faintly hear, while the other dangled down the right side of his chest.

"What happened, José? Is everything alright?" I asked. "The police stopped me," he said, pulling out a piece of paper, a ticket for $250. José was so shaken up he hadn't even read it. The ticket said he was fined for running a red light.

I explained to him, "It says you were fined for driving through a red light even though you were already stopped." José looked confused. José then told us that when the police berries started flashing red and blue in his rearview mirror, he panicked as he pulled over to the side of the road, worried that perhaps he might have broken a law he was unaware of which would potentially jeopardize his residency status. I could understand where his anxiety was coming from though. His residency was still in a probationary period and the thought of him attempting to head back to Cuba using his current car as a canoe would not go down well (actually, that's exactly where it would go based on the current condition of that junker).

After we reassured him that his residency was not at risk and that he only had to pay a fine, his cheery self came back to life. He told us a parable in broken English about making mistakes and learning from them, that didn't really make sense, but we understood what he was getting at. He was also very adamant that he would never drive through a red light, which we believed because he was the most respectful guy you'd ever met who just wanted to do right by himself and everybody around him. Feeling more relieved, he sat down at his workstation and turned up his music, bald head bobbing back and forth as he got down to work. It wasn't until I walked over to his workstation that I was able to connect the dots.

As I neared José's cubicle, I could hear the "Red light, Green light" song blasting from his headphones, again. He had been listening to this song in his car on his way to work. As he was sitting at the traffic lights, the speakers blurted, "Green Light!" His associations between the colour of the traffic light and the words in the song must have become entangled. That's when he drove through the red light straight into the middle of the intersection.

I explained my theory to him. José sat there in silence, the wheels of wonder in obvious motion. His eyes widened with realization and he began to laugh hysterically. Then, he gave the best self-help advice I've ever heard. With earnestness, he solemnly declared, "From now on, I will only listen to podcasts in the car."

José promised that he would take extreme precaution driving from here on out, and I had every confidence in him that he would arrive at work the following Saturday without breaking any more laws.

INTERNATIONAL MAN OF MYSTERY
~ For Kaitlyn ~

I grew up moving a lot. Not just schools, but cities and provinces, too. This was due to a combination of variables like my parents changing professions and looking for more opportunities outside of Manitoba. By the time I was done high school, I had attended nine different schools. There are pros and cons that come with moving so much. A few of the benefits are increased adaptability, resilience, and flexibility. There were many opportunities and doors to walk through that would never have been an option had we not moved. For that, I am thankful and have no regrets.

The cons were definitely relational. So much uprooting left me feeling like I just couldn't build solid friendships that naturally take time, trust and continuity of some sort. I was always starting from scratch and by the time high school rolled around, I was far more apprehensive when it came to making new friends. For most of my teenage years, I was part of the same church and developed friendships there. We had shared values and faith and we enjoyed seeing each other every week. None of my church friends went to school with me, so I was always looking forward to the end of the day when I could hang out with my true friends. I got along with people in high school and had enough social skills to be friendly and do work projects together if needed, but they never amounted to anything more than acquaintances. I realize it takes two to tango where relationships are concerned, but being of Mennonite descent,

I was not much interested in dancing.

When grade eleven rolled around, I started at a new high school (again), in a town north of Toronto. The school population had clearly defined social groups and cliques that I couldn't quite break into. It was around this time that I had a pretty heavy obsession with Ukraine, Russia and Eastern Europe My love for that part of the world was reinforced by my childhood addiction to the Nintendo 64 game, "Goldeneye," which had me playing endless mission hours as James Bond when I should have been doing my homework. If you haven't seen the Goldeneye movie, a majority of it takes place in the Soviet Union and features a lot of Russian accents. It was, in many ways, an inaccurate portrayal of Russia, but it sparked an intrigue for all things Eastern European, which remains with me to this day.

Two weeks into grade eleven, as I was adjusting to my new surroundings, I grew weary at the thought of trying to fit into a new social group. The investment of putting myself out there, being vulnerable and losing newly made friends seemed too much to risk. I'd done that before several times over only to move away and start again.

Most of the kids at my new school had known each other since elementary school, and it showed. Some of these kids had dated each other, others played hockey in the same league, and others were early childhood friends whose families were quite close. All of these kids had been friends or enemies at one time or another and I was jealous because I never got to experience that kind of long-lasting relationship dynamic in a school setting. I knew I'd never be one of them and my eyes were set on the prize of finishing high school so I could go travelling. Rather than be resentful about it, I committed to accepting it for what it was and continued to move forward, making the best of it.

I'm not sure if it was intentional or some sort of bizarre psychological defence mechanism that kicked in, but I developed a persona to avoid having to deal with the pressures of making new friends.

I had a buzz cut, I was into soccer and wore Adidas clothing, and I was learning the Russian alphabet because I was planning to travel there later that year. One day, without much thought, someone asked me a question and a Russian accent blurted out of my mouth. Before I knew it, my peers thought English was my second language and they didn't care to include me since they didn't think I could understand much of what they were saying. I used this facade as an excuse to avoid pursuing relationships with my classmates. It was a win/win situation, I figured.

The ESL (English as a second language) table in the cafeteria was made up of students who spoke different languages as their primary language. Conversations were very basic, and more was said through eye contact and facial expressions than words since nobody understood each other anyway. As an ESL imposter, I was welcomed into the foreigner fold. The exchange students and immigrants were my people; we were an adoptive family of misfits that didn't really know each other.

As a psychotherapist, I see children with social anxiety that often turns to school refusal. Looking back now, I'm able to see that taking on this unassuming role was my way of dealing with this social anxiety while still being able to meet my responsibilities of attending class.

I think my grades that year were the highest they'd ever been because I wasn't distracted by school friends and the associated shenanigans that would come with them. I would head home after school and hang out with my real friends, from church, who had no idea that grade eleven was a double life for me. As soon as I walked out of those school doors at three-thirty in the afternoon, the Russian disguise would come off.

I was thrown a curveball near the end of grade eleven, when a new student joined our school. He was a recently landed immigrant, fleeing from war torn Chechnya with his sister and parents. Like a moth to one of those bright blue bug zappers, Khabib ended up finding the ESL lunch table in the cafeteria and befriended me.

Khabib spoke broken English, but his sister, who also sat at the ESL table, spoke better English and would translate some of what I would say to him and vice versa. I didn't want him to realize I was an ESL imposter, so I gradually changed my accent, making it seem as though my English abilities had progressed leaps and bounds.

As a refugee, Khabib had clearly seen some heavy stuff back in Chechnya. I found out from his sister that he was actually two years older, but they decided to put him in our grade because it would help with social integration and it matched his academic level, on account of gaps he experienced in his education due to the war.

One day, in phys-ed class, Khabib joined us for a shirts versus skins outdoor soccer game. Khabib knew soccer, a universal sport, and our gym coach put him on my team. Khabib took off his shirt and all the classmates were stunned. He had huge biceps and a ripped six pack. He was a real life G.I. Joeski. When the soccer game started, he was leaping through the air, doing spin kicks and dribbling figure eight's around the other team. The rest of our team attempted to play defense, even though there was no need for it. Even our coach was shocked at his skill. I'm not sure what phys-ed in Chechnya looks like, but if Khabib showed us anything, it's that those "arm circle" warm ups we would do at the start of each class were pretty useless.

Back in the cafeteria one day, I asked Khabib's sister where he learned to play soccer, and how he got those biceps. I was able to decipher from her answers that most Chechens play soccer from a young age and that he obtained his physique from fighting in the Chechen war against the Russians. He had full combat training and his role specifically was a "rocket launcher infantryman."

Chechnya was on the defence against Russia in those years (the late 90s and early 2000's), and they had Chechen boys as young as fourteen fighting for their homeland. Chechen animosity towards the Russians had grown quite strong and it was at this point in hearing her explanation that I made a very clear distinction to Khabib and his sister that while I knew a bit of the Russian alphabet and few phrases, my ethnicity was actually more Ukrainian and Mennonite and I didn't really have any ties to Russia, lest I push the wrong buttons on this Chechen. She smiled and Khabib chuckled.

For those last few months of school, I took Khabib and his sister everywhere with me. I ate with them, hung out with them at breaks, and helped them with homework. I ended up learning a lot about Chechnya and Russian culture and gained a unique perspective on their situation. Khabib and his sister were my closest friends at school that year. Near the end of the semester, the school social worker who was assigned to Khabib when he came to Canada flagged me down in the hallway and thanked me for making Khabib and his sister feel welcome and included. The irony was not lost on me. I was an ambassador of welcome to somewhere I felt no belonging to.

In hindsight, that eleventh year of school taught me an unexpected lesson, which was that one of the easiest ways to make friends is to welcome the unwelcome. Maybe if I'd let my guard down earlier in the year, I could have allowed someone to welcome me in the same way. I'm still trying to decide whether this entire story is a tragedy or a highly successful experiment in how to cope with relationship anxiety. I've reframed it as the latter.

BOLDLY GOING WHERE WE'LL NEVER GO AGAIN
~ For Michelle B. ~

Ben, my good friend, and I, had our small travel sized suitcases packed and we were about to head to Calgary from Toronto. We were longtime *Star Trek: The Next Generation* fans and a once in a lifetime opportunity came up that we couldn't turn down. The entire original cast of *TNG* would reunite on stage for the first time in 25 years at the Calgary Comic Expo. If you purchased your tickets early enough, you'd have the rare chance to have your photo taken with all the cast members, including Captain Jean-Luc Picard. A photo-op with Picard likely wouldn't come around again.

We spent significant portions of our childhood watching *TNG* episodes. Watching them in the evening made us feel like we were part of whatever syndicated adventure happened to be running that week. To this day, I like to view it in the evening with the lights off to enhance the stellar ambience. *TNG* became a source of expected comfort, with the predictable single mission episode formats and the gentle hum of the Enterprise D's warp engines running in the background.

With 40 minutes left till departure, Ben and I slowly shuffled our way down the aisle, careful not to bump anyone on the way to our seats. Some people were sitting, others were looking out the windows and playing with the air conditioning nozzles and lights above their heads, while others were putting their luggage into the overhead compartments.

Calgary is 3113 km from Toronto, and it takes approximately three hours to travel there by plane. Unfortunately, Ben and I couldn't afford to fly there so we took the Greyhound Bus. It takes 53 hours and 30 minutes to travel that same distance on a Greyhound Bus. For scale, that is the equivalent of driving from Paris, France to Moscow, Russia. With our eye on the Picard prize, we were not deterred by the long journey ahead. We were young and adventurous, we rationalized.

53 hours in a Greyhound bus is like being caught in a temporal anomaly. Once I finished reading my book and watching my Netflix show (we only had wireless internet for three out of the 50 hours) and exhausted my conversation time, I began to enter a forced state of deep contemplation. I looked out the window and scanned the scenery as it whizzed by (infinite trees and lakes) and it served the purpose of periodic hypnosis to kill the time.

Eventually, I turned my gaze towards the inside of the bus and analyzed the entire interior. The blue seat fabric, the diagonal patterns embedded in it, the rubber grooves in the aisle floor, the reflection of the driver's face in his large dashboard mirror. To keep my neck from getting stiff, I oscillated my head from the interior view back towards the window, rinsed and repeated for 53 hours.

Sitting for too long made me tired, but the inconvenience of sitting upright and the bumpiness of the twists and turns meant I couldn't sleep for more than an hour. As such, I'd frequently drift in and out of consciousness. Any time I'd wake up from a light sleep, I'd have a kink in my neck or lose feeling in one of my limbs. Well into the journey, one lady near the front of the bus stood up to stretch and her leg gave out due to a cramp, ending with a large crash on the floor. Thankfully, her large inflatable neck pillow broke her fall. The bus driver stared forward as if nothing happened. The Greyhound stops for no one.

With each hour that passed, the decency of the passengers began a quick decline into degeneracy. At one of the hundreds of points in the journey, I got up to walk up and down the aisle to stretch my legs. I saw an older lady in one seat who looked like she was in a comatose state. Her head was drooped forward in her seat and there was a puddle of her drool collecting on the floor between her legs. When the bus driver slammed on the brakes to avoid colliding with several deer, her head was thrown backwards into her seat. She was still asleep though, perhaps in a real coma now. Food and drink were launched from people's hands onto the floor. People were startled. There was no acknowledgment from the bus driver, whose gaze remained forward as he continued to drive. The Greyhound must continue.

As with most busses, the toilet was way at the back. Some people stayed in that washroom far longer than was reasonable. Sometimes I could hear laughter coming from within. Sometimes flatulence. Sometimes both at the same time. Any time someone would exit the bathroom, they would crop dust a combination of air freshener, Axe body spray and marijuana throughout the aisle for all to inhale. The bus driver never once stopped to pee. Maybe he was just desperate to get to his destination so he wouldn't have to stay on the bus longer than necessary?

Every so often I would look at my watch to see how much time was left on the journey. I then tried a game where I'd withhold looking at the time for as long as possible, figuring that it might make the trip feel like it was going by more quickly. It never worked.

One of the more dramatic moments on the journey happened in the middle of the night. There was a large bald man who took up an entire row to himself, seated in the middle of the bus. He was drinking out of a very large plastic bottle for most of the bus drive, and it must have contained vodka in it because as the trip progressed, he became more impaired and impulsive. Around 3 am, he started walking around the bus and tried talking to people who were asleep by tapping their shoulders and engaging in one-sided conversations. Maybe he'd done this trip before, and knew he couldn't do it without alcohol? I'd certainly understand if that was the case. About 10 hours into the journey and you begin to feel insanely claustrophobic and restless due to the limited entertainment and terrible sleep.

In any event, this man had more than he could handle and began lurching his body up the aisle to use the bathroom, stumbling along the way. If this were a Star Trek episode, it could have been a scene on the bridge where everyone falls over after being hit by a photon torpedo. When he came out of the bathroom, he had no pants on. Only his underwear and a t-shirt. He slurred something about it being too hot and not being able to find his cat.

He was so ham sauced that he fell over and cut his head on the side of a passenger's elbow rest. She gave a startled reaction, not knowing if the man meant harm or not. A passenger saw blood dripping from his head and offered him a bandage. The bald guy put the bandage on the side of his head where there was no wound and he fell asleep face down right there in the aisle. So close, and yet so far from his seat. Little did he know, his journey to the bathroom and back would foreshadow our entire bus ride. The bus driver ignored the entire debacle. He was one with the Greyhound. Nothing could stop him from his continuing mission.

The bald man lay asleep on the floor for two hours, which brought us to a pit stop in Winnipeg. As soon as the bus stopped, police boarded and forcefully removed him. The bus driver watched them arrest him from his dashboard mirror, not turning his head once. The bald guy told the police that they had no right to take him off the bus and separate him from his family. An officer then asked for this man's family to raise their hands to identify themselves, and no one did. We're not sure if he lied or his family was too embarrassed to be associated with him. As we waited for the bus to get going again, we could hear the man singing the national anthem to the police officers outside.

For the remainder of the ride, the smells became worse, the aches and pains more intense, and heightened sensitivity to annoying noises off the charts, but at some point, you get a "Greyhound high" and find the will to keep going. You have no other choice. The Greyhound must go on.

When the bus arrived at the Calgary terminal and we finally got off, it felt like we had just returned home from the Eastern Front in WW2. Our eyes were bloodshot from poor sleep and our bodies fatigued. People stumbled down the Greyhound stairs and onto the ground. I never appreciated a hotel bed and hot meal as much as I did after getting off that bus.

After that trip, I didn't want to see another bald head ever again. But the next day, as we approached Patrick Stewart and his skull- all shiny and shorn, any apprehension for follically challenged individuals immediately melted away. We walked over to his side and told him that it was an honour to meet him. "The honour is all mine," he replied back, in his smooth baritone voice. His gaze never broke focus, staring forward at the camera much like he would if he were staring into the viewscreen of the Enterprise D's bridge. Alas, after an exhausting journey we met the Captain, our childhood dreams fulfilled. It was a delirious sojourn, yes, but the prize was worth every minute.

I'm not sure who created the transporter technology in *Star Trek*, but I would not be surprised if that person was motivated to do so after travelling a long distance on a Greyhound bus.

IN THE BEGINNING WAS SEGA
~ For Lyla ~

Back in 1994, I was living with my younger brother and mother in a small apartment building in Winnipeg, Manitoba. My mom was a single mom for two years by this point and was working multiple jobs to pay the bills. Life wasn't easy in those early years for a variety of factors, but her hard work and care for us never went unnoticed. I was aware at seven years old that we did not have a lot of money and in hindsight, that didn't really bother me too much because we had a very supportive family and church community, and our needs were met.

That year, my mom planned a birthday party for me at the McDonald's Playplace and invited some of my friends and family members. All the kids received their own Happy Meals and were free to run around the play centre and enjoy themselves. When it came time to open birthday presents, I opened my mom's gift last. I remember that the wrapping paper was red, and it was in the shape of a large square box that felt quite heavy.

As I slowly tore away the wrapping paper, I could see the image of a blue hedgehog wearing red shoes with a mischievous grin looking back at me. Next to him was this orange little fox with two tails, and a black machine with two controllers that had a directional pad and three buttons (A, B and C).

My mom had bought me my very first video game console, the "SEGA GENESIS" with the video game, "Sonic the Hedgehog 2."

To this day, it is the most memorable and special gift I've ever received. My mom was able to buy it on discount from one of the grocery stores that she worked at. Kids shouldn't have to worry about the financial situation of their parents, but I did, and knowing the position my mom was in made me value this gift all the more.

If things in life were tough, the SEGA Genesis provided me and my brother countless hours of fun and escapism where we could join Sonic and Tails in their adventures to defeat the evil Dr. Robotnik through a variety of spellbinding levels with catchy tunes that I can remember to this day. Flip the switch on the machine and you'd be hit with the TV speakers and loud iconic sound so many people from the early '90s remember, "Saayy-gaaaah" in its giant blue block lettering that covered most of the screen.

Everyone at my age was either a Nintendo or a SEGA fan, and even if you enjoyed the games and characters from both game systems, you always had one that you pledged loyalty to. For me, hands down, it was SEGA, and Sonic the Hedgehog in particular.

As the years went on and new technology and advances in video gaming happened, SEGA would be left in the dust, much like Sonic would leave his foes, ironically. But, I'd always retain this nostalgic appreciation for the character, the gaming system and the sacrifice it was for my mother to purchase it for me.

Several years ago I decided to visit Tokyo on a short flight from Korea because I had a few vacation days I was required to use up from my teaching job. I had a friend living in Tokyo and thought I'd quickly visit him and his wife, as well as make a pilgrimage to the SEGA building headquarters (where Sonic was created) as a tribute trip for all the fun childhood memories it gave me.

If I had to do it again, I would have made my trip longer because there's too much going on in Japan for a two day visit. Tokyo specifically, is overwhelming for all the five senses and there's so much to take in and process. In Japan, everything is cute and weird, ancient and modern. There's really no other place in the world and the way these contrasts all interact is quite unique.

Upon arriving in Tokyo, you feel like you are in a real life video game. There are so many different places to go, bright colours to see, and the instructions for how to get around aren't super clear on what you need to do, where you need to go or how you can even get there. You just have to keep moving and hope you end up in the right place. It's quite overwhelming. As soon as you land at Haneda International Airport, you enter problem-solving mode fast. *Where is customs clearance? Can I use a bathroom first? Oh dear Lord, how do I use this toilet? What will happen if I push one of these twenty-five buttons on it? Wait... is this even a toilet?*

Even Tokyo's extensive train network is reminiscent of a map in video games that you need to look at in order to navigate correctly. The Tokyo subway map is a massive labyrinth of multi-coloured lines and station stops with unpronounceable names that raise the journey difficulty from a medium to a hard. *Which part of the city should I explore first? Do I go up, down, left or right?* These are the thoughts that assaulted my mind as I had to decide what to do in a short space of time with no knowledge of the Japanese language.

Tired from trying to understand the subway map, I figured it was time to get some food since I hadn't eaten in several hours. There was a vending machine over there to my right and as I approached I noticed there were forty different drinks to choose from, all with weird names that didn't help me understand what I'd actually be drinking. Do I try the "Pocari Sweat" or a drink called "Coolpis" with a picture of cabbage on it? Or a brown bottle called "Bilk" which is 70% milk, 30% beer and 100% disgusting? How come water isn't an option? These are the thoughts running through my head at turbo speed that I can't share out loud because I'm travelling alone.

I settle on the "Pocari Sweat" drink which ends up tasting a little like Gatorade (thankfully) and I begin to munch on a snack bar made out of peanut butter I found in the adjacent vending machine. You shouldn't have to take forty-five minutes to select snacks from a Japanese vending machine, but they don't really give you any other choice when it presents you with endless options. Tokyo is known as the vending machine capital of the world, offering the most unique and bizarre items. Farm fresh eggs, vegetables, bananas, cigarettes, liquor, books, umbrellas, condoms, lingerie, feminine hygiene products, toilet paper and even diapers. I even saw a vending machine that allows you to buy dogs, yes, actual dogs. The list goes on. If you can imagine it, Tokyo's probably got a vending machine for it.

When I finally see signs for a train station, I make my way over to it and take out my paper map in an attempt to locate which train I need to take to get to my hotel. I move towards the platform and pray that I get on the right train and that it goes in the right direction. Surely, it can't be that difficult to follow the map and end up at the right station where my hotel is? Japanese efficiency is world-renowned, but only if you're relatively proficient in Japanese, which I am not.

The platform has people queued in an orderly fashion, most people in business suit attire, staring at their phones while they wait for their trains that are never late. As we wait on the platform, I can hear the sound of birds chirping, but I can see no birds anywhere. I found out later that they do this intentionally to manipulate how people think while they are waiting to go to work. Researchers decided to include bird noises on speakers everywhere on the platform because there is evidence to suggest that hearing them reduces stress and anxiety.

When my train finally pulls up for arrival, it is packed! Everyone in the queue appears to pack themselves inside though, which makes no sense because there is seemingly no room for more people. There are legs and hands hanging out of the doors as they try to close, clamping down on their limbs. Train attendants wearing white gloves are hired to stand there and shove the protruding limbs back into the train so the door can close and the train can resume. It's a claustrophobic nightmare for Westerners, but just another day for the Japanese who didn't seem to notice or care.

I decide I'll wait for the next train, which will hopefully be a little less packed. However, it ends up being just as packed and the queue is just as long, and again, the Japanese all manage to get in. I couldn't figure out how! I'll wait for the next one after that, I thought, going back to the queue again with my head lowered in sadness like Charlie Brown. Forty-five minutes later, I miss ten train entry opportunities and realize that it won't get any less empty. So, I commit to forcing myself on. Getting into that Japanese subway train reminded me a lot of a young child who encounters an escalator for the first time and makes multiple attempts to get on before circling back and allowing everyone else to get on first, while they wait and observe how to do it.

I tried to push myself into the train like a sumo wrestler tries to shove his opponent. Then, I wondered silently whether or not they ever hired sumo wrestlers for the role of being a train platform attendant. They'd be perfect for that role. I can feel everyone breathing on me, there's no personal space, and the passengers all have this look on their face that says, "It is what it is." I struggle to contain a burp but let one out softly. It smells like Gatorade and peanut butter, the remnants of my vending machine snack from earlier. I look around at the faces inches away from mine, expecting them to react to the smell, but they don't flinch. I am impressed by their emotionless postures. I wonder, silently, if they are secretly thinking horrible thoughts about my burp or if they genuinely don't care. It bothers me that I'll never know. If they had spoken English, I probably would have asked them.

We get to the next station stop, which I know because a unique jingle begins to play throughout the train speakers. As you arrive at each station stop, you are welcomed with a unique seven second tune that plays throughout the subway and station. The short songs are created by a famous composer with a synthesizer and it always sounds cute and upbeat, again, reminding you of being in a video game where each level has a different theme tune that you begin to associate with that level. As soon as those songs stop, the fake bird chirping resumes throughout the platform.

More people board the train, and I get shoved further into the abyss of the car and black business suits. I can feel my anxiety rising and feel I am close to having a panic attack. My mind begins to race with thoughts like, *What happens when I get to my stop? How the heck do I get out of here? What if these people take offence to my shoving? Aren't most people in Japan trained in martial arts from a young age? I don't want to get beaten up.* I manage to tune into the rhythm of all the bodies in the train, like a bee in a hive and am able to slowly push my way to the exit with no altercations. Even the chaos in Japan, as it turns out, functions in an orderly way.

I finally arrive at my intended station. It's nighttime now but you wouldn't know it from the bright lights and billboards that are plastered over every building. I can see my hotel, one purposely picked for its close proximity to the station so I wouldn't have trouble finding it. It's been a long day and my brain is fried from having to focus so much. I can't wait to get a good night's sleep in a comfy bed. The following morning, I'd get to see my long-lost friend and visit the SEGA headquarters in Shinagawa City, a suburb of Tokyo.

The attendant at the hotel entrance bowed to welcome me and brought me to a little room with a locker where she said I could put my bag, shoes and any other items I have. *Why can't I just keep this all in my hotel room?* I thought. Must be a Japanese thing, I concluded. She then escorts me to my room and opens a door to a long hallway. She tells me that my room is "B15."

As it turns out, I don't get my own room. The so-called hotel room I booked is actually a wall full of pods a little larger than a coffin where you are to sleep. They are called "capsule hotels" and are one of Japan's best known and unique types of lodging. They are found around major train stations in large cities and appeal to individuals looking for a low budget, single night's stay. On both sides of the long hallway are two levels of capsules, basically the ultimate of bunk bedrooms. The capsule has a thin tatami mattress, a blanket, pillow, a little air conditioning panel and a small TV built into the roof to watch before bed. The only privacy is a wooden bamboo shutter blind that you can pull down and hook onto the floor.

The sleep wasn't too bad. Nobody speaks to one another, the only sound you can hear is everyone snoring and there's a slight smell of beer in the air, from the businessmen who go drinking after work and then crash in their capsules late at night.

When I wake up the following morning, I go to the communal bathroom to brush my teeth and then head to an eating area within the motel where I am served an odd breakfast (a boiled egg, a steamed hot dog wiener, some french fries and a fermented radish). If I had Twitter back then, I would have tweeted an image of it to show off how pathetic it looked. I scarf it down and pack up my things to continue my journey to find my friend and the SEGA headquarters. I have to get back on the subway again, but this time I'm more prepared for what to expect.

That would be my only night sleeping in the capsule hotel as I'd have to fly back to Korea really late that same evening. I was heading to Akihabara Station to meet my friend, the infamous electronics district in Tokyo, and saw a small paper ad for the district in the capsule hotel. It had pictures of all these cool buildings, one of which had a giant blue SEGA sign, easily recognizable to me. SEGA is quite popular all over Japan, because not only did they make the Genesis gaming system that I grew up with, they are also responsible for most of the arcade games you see around the world. So, seeing their bright blue logo there is akin to seeing the yellow McDonald's "M" in North America.

My battery on my phone was low and I texted my friend to say that I'd be arriving at Akihabara district and I told him that we should meet by the blue SEGA sign on the main street, just like I'd seen in the ad at the hotel. It was an obvious landmark for me to point out. He responded with a "thumbs up" icon and said he couldn't wait to see me and take me out for high quality ramen noodles. Akihabara is Tokyo's main shopping district for video games, anime, manga, electronics and computer-related items and is extremely busy, something I hadn't realized before deciding to meet him there.

As I walked from the train station to the main street in Akihabara district, I was horrified as I realized that there were blue SEGA signs everywhere and on almost every building. Telling my friend to meet me by the blue SEGA sign might as well have been like asking him to meet me by "that guy standing over there." It was a needle in a haystack, and to make matters worse, my phone had now died, leaving me unable to call him to set a different meeting point.

I tried walking to different buildings with SEGA signs to see if he was there, but I couldn't find him. I didn't know what to do. It was like being on a "Where's Waldo?" page where they insert multiple Waldo's to confuse you. I waited for two hours and my friend never appeared. I did not want to risk finding the headquarters on my own, lest I get lost in the Tokyo vortex yet again. My flight time was fast approaching and I ended up having to get my train back to Haneda Airport without finding my friend or the headquarters. I'd find out after the trip that we were both trying to find one another under different SEGA signs, assuming the other person would linger in the same spot.

It was game over. I couldn't find my friend or pay homage to the origins of my favourite blue hedgehog. There was no option to "try again" because this was real life and not a video game, sadly. While I failed at my mission, I did enjoy the experience of attempting to complete it. Just like my childhood, I don't actually remember completing my Sonic the Hedgehog game successfully, I only remember how much fun I had trying.

A SIGN FROM HEAVEN
~ For Hannah ~

The city of Bath is the most beautiful city I've ever lived in, bar none. It's where my wife was born and raised and the story of how I came there is a sign and a wonder in its own right. Bath is a small gem nestled in the Southwest of England, about two hours west of London. Many Europeans have heard of Bath, but the average North American hasn't.

The people of Bath are known for having a "posh" accent, unlike the rest of Somerset which has more of a farmer accent. The Bath accent matches the upper-class feel of the city. When travelling to Bath, you move through rich emerald hills (the typical rolling English countryside dotted with sheep) and then all of a sudden, like an oasis in a desert, Bath appears. You can't miss it. There are no skyscrapers, bright city lights or obscene landmarks distracting you from the natural beauty. Bath blends into the countryside in an organic way, and a lot of that has to do with the creamy complexions of the buildings.

Most, if not all the buildings in Bath are made from Bath Stone, a specific type of limestone from the region. This stone has a warm earthy hue that contrasts against the backdrop of the surrounding green grassy hills. When the sun sets, the stone turns a warm honey colour as it reflects the orange street lamps that illuminate the cobblestone streets.

The geography of the city is as layered as the history within it. There are many steep hills, and the houses and buildings are often staggered to accommodate the land. In between these buildings are narrow staircases connecting to other streets and corridors. It feels like a maze that you don't want to find the exit to. The entire city is walkable, and that is part of its charm (you are also never more than a few hundred feet away from a pub).

The buildings also span incredible time periods. Bath is almost 2,000 years old, being founded in the first century AD by the Romans as they expanded into Britain. The Romans settled in Bath because of its natural hot springs that have legendary healing properties. Above ground, the medieval architecture (the Bath Abbey) can be seen. This abbey was where the very first King of England was crowned. It had previously been an Anglo-Saxon monastery that was torn down by the Normans, then rebuilt into the Abbey that currently stands there today.

You could say that the Bath Stone is a storyteller on its own, for everywhere you walk there is a building that has a story to tell, which is why walking the streets of the city never seems to get boring. There is always something new to discover.

I moved to Bath when I was 18, in pursuit of both a girl (my wife now) and some ministry roles I was considering. Before I became a teacher and now a psychotherapist, I was strongly contemplating becoming a pastor. I was granted a visa to live and work in England for two years and flew over with little to no plan. Making that decision was a bit of a process though, and it wasn't a rational decision based on logic. I've learned that sometimes these are the best decisions, when the heart knows best before the head does.

Prior to moving to England, I kept asking God whether I should move there. During that time, I had many dreams at night that involved white horses. This was strange as I didn't have any particular interest or connection to horses, let alone white horses. One day as I was sitting at a friend's house, I found this coffee table book called *Aerial Views of England*. I opened the first page, and there before me was a picture of a giant white horse carved out of stone, etched into some hills. I was trying not to read into it too much. I know that love is blind, and I really liked my future wife, but I couldn't differentiate between blind love and confirmation bias and what was possibly "God's leading."

My mind would play these tug of war games where I'd talk myself out of viewing a white horse as some sort of sign to move to

England, and then in other moments, my heart would convince me that throughout history God has spoken to people in various ways. Maybe, just maybe, this white horse thing was a nudge from above.

At the time, it felt risky and borderline delusional, but I grew up in a very Charismatic Christian culture that placed a great emphasis on signs and wonders and God speaking in bizarre ways. In the end, I rationalized that I was 18, and the worst thing that could happen was that I'd be wrong and England would not be the right decision, and maybe I should get my head checked out by a doctor.

When my plane landed in London, and I drove the two hours to Bath, I'd end up driving past that same white horse (the Westbury White Horse) I saw in the coffee table book several months prior. That sealed the deal for me.

When I arrived, I applied for a job running a mailroom at a local ministry. On my walk to the interview, I passed a pub called the White Horse. Sure enough, I ended up being offered the job on the spot. Logic and reason would say that moving to England when you are 18, uneducated and hyper-spiritual, shouldn't go well. In this case, moving to Bath was an adventure in faith, and seeing all my needs provided for during the four years I ended up living there. I shudder just thinking about what my life would look like today, had I not moved to England.

Alas, I'm sharing how I came to Bath because this story is more about how we came to the conclusion to leave the city, a more difficult decision, it would turn out, than choosing to go there in the first place.

My wife and I lived on Milsom Street, one of the high streets in downtown Bath. Jane Austen had made this same street her home in the early 1800s and wrote about Bath in her novels. She is probably the most famous person connected to Bath, but there are many notable people from history who have made their home there.

The office where I worked had noticeable scrapes and cuts on the outside of the building. In fact, many buildings throughout Bath that weren't newly built had indentations that I would never have noticed until my father-in-law pointed it out one day. It turns out that the Nazis did air raids on Bath in April of 1942 for 2 days straight and many of the scars you see on buildings today, came from Nazi aircraft. It was called the "Bath Blitz' and it took most of the people off guard. The city was chosen as a target for its cultural and historical significance rather than having any strategic or military value.

In one weekend, Bath suffered three raids from Nazi aircraft, which took off from Nazi occupied northern France. Bath emergency sirens wailed, but few people took cover because they assumed the bombers were headed for the neighbouring port city of Bristol (far more strategically relevant than Bath). The bombers flew low to drop explosives and then returned to rake the streets with machine-gun fire before flying back across the English Channel to refuel and do the same thing all over again. It would have been terrifying living in Bath at that time.

The attacks happened in the middle of the night, killing 400 people, injuring many more and damaging 19,000 buildings - many of which show scars to this day.

Every time I walked to work, I thought about how just 65 years earlier the streets were a war zone. I would try to imagine myself running for cover as the city lit up, not with its iconic orange street lights of today, but with the orange glow of fires spreading across the city. I just couldn't imagine it though - it was and still is too foreign a concept for me.

One day, during our third year in Bath, Hannah and I were out walking the streets. Against the backdrop of all the history and beauty, we were having a heated argument. We were arguing about whether we should continue living in Bath or move back to Canada. I'd lived in England for almost four years by this point, and the country had really grown on me. We had a great community of family, friends and church and I felt really lucky to be there. I loved the adventure of living in a new place.

In contrast, Hannah had lived in Bath her entire life and was itching for some adventure. She wanted to break out of the comfortability of all she'd known and make a new path for herself. It had become quite a bone of contention between us for several months as we weighed the pros and cons of staying in England while balancing our dreams and aspirations as a couple.

The argument began to get a little more animated, and since we didn't want to draw attention to ourselves in the middle of the street, we walked down to a quieter side street and sat down on a bench to continue our conversation. We proceeded to argue and were getting nowhere. I wanted to stay, and she wanted to leave. It was the first time being married that I really felt like we were at a really problematic impasse. There was a long pause as we came to a standstill. In frustration, I exclaimed, "I wish God could just tell us what to do! I don't like having to make big decisions like this. Maybe He'll give us a sign like when I first decided to move here?"

Not 15 seconds later, a pigeon crapped all over Hannah's head. I burst into laughter, thinking I had won the argument and the pigeon was a prophetic sign from God that we were to stay in England. She challenged my interpretation, proposing that this was an indicator that if we stayed in Bath it would be crappy for her.

In the end, her interpretation won out. If a white horse had ridden past us during that argument, maybe we'd still be in Bath today. However, we both felt at peace about moving back to Canada after four wonderful years soaking up all we could in Bath. And like our time in Bath, our every need has been taken care of back in Canada where we continue to be led by heart and faith for big decisions that make us uncomfortable. There's no way I'd rather live

IT'S NOT EASY BEING GREEN
~ For Tyler ~

A couple of days ago, Hannah took our sons down to the creek that connects to our local waterfall. I was at work, and when they came home the boys were noticeably excited to tell me that they had seen four frogs while they were there. We had been living in the area for a year and we hadn't seen a frog once, so I was impressed.

My sons' excitement reminded me of when I was a kid and we would visit my grandparent's cottage on the border of Manitoba and Ontario. My grandma and grandpa built their cabin with their bare hands. They trekked the lumber, nails, hammers and saws through some pretty heavy brush and constructed a beautiful wooden cabin on a quiet lake that they would enjoy for many years.

The surrounding landscape was beautiful. We were encompassed by forest, the smell of dirt, the sound of moving water and the fire pit cackling where we'd bake fish we caught in the lake and roast marshmallows. A small hike up behind the cottage led to a field of delicious wild blueberries, which we could pick at leisure. We had to be careful when picking them though because bear poop looked exactly like stepped-on blueberries and it would have been an unfortunate mistake to confuse the two. Naturally, knowing that bears and wolves could be in the forest, contained us kids, since we were always just fearful enough not to wander too far.

One of our favourite things to do out there was play in a small creek near the cabin. This creek was crystal clear and the water was still and shallow enough to play in. In this creek lived many frogs, something that was rather appealing to young boys like me and my younger brother Tyler. Even more appealing was the fact that these frogs weren't particularly fast, so we could scoop our hands into the water to catch them. A lot of our time was spent in pursuit of these slippery little creatures.

One day, Tyler and I were playing together in the water. Armed with a bucket, my brother was eagerly searching for some frogs and rocks to scoop up. Wanting to explore more, Tyler asked if he could go and play in the shallow waters of the beach. I told him it was OK, as long as he didn't go past his belly button and I could still see him from the shore. He agreed not to stray too far as he happily skipped away.

I continued to wade through the creek, looking for frogs and any other cool rocks while frequently checking to ensure he wasn't going too far. As the older sibling, I was commissioned with the responsibility of watching over my carefree brother.

I could see Tyler in the distance, wading into the water with his bucket that was floating beside him. One by one, Tyler removed a rock from his bucket and threw it as high in the air as he could before it came back down to hit the water. Not one to miss out on some good old fashioned rock throwing, I ran over to join him (I also figured this would be the perfect opportunity to show him how much higher I could throw the rocks than he could-typical older brother stuff).

As I got closer, I could see quite clearly that he wasn't throwing rocks in the air; he was hurling his frogs in the air. He had a look of pure delight and glee as the frogs soared into the sky. "Tyler! What are you doing?!" I exclaimed. He looked at me, confusion on his face. I continued, "You're throwing the frogs high into the air, they are fragile, I think you killed them!"

"No I didn't. Look, they're fine." Tyler, in his innocence, looked genuinely clueless about what he had done. His smile gradually faded from a Joker-like grin to that iconic disappointed look Mr. Bean gives when he's realized he's made a huge mistake. Floating around him like the last few soggy cheerios in a bowl of milk, were the frogs, clearly dead and bloated from impact. He hadn't realized the power of his own strength and the fragility of these little creatures.

I had him pick the frogs up and showed him that there was no longer life in them, the victims of an unexpected launch towards the heavens, only to be re-traumatized on the way down, smacking the water like cement. My brother was like Godzilla to these amphibians. He looked more defensive than guilty because I was clearly scolding him, and he knew he would be in trouble if my parents found out.

Out of respect for the animals, and because I was charged with keeping an eye on him, I told Tyler that he would have to pick up all five of the dead frogs and bring them back to the creek from whence they came. I instructed him to dig five small holes to bury each one individually and with his plastic toy shovel in hand, Tyler went to work. "You don't have to watch me do it, I'll do it myself" he said. I agreed to give him some privacy and said I would come back in 10 minutes to check on him. I began walking away but wanted to ensure he followed my instructions. So, I hid behind a large tree and peered around the side to monitor what he was doing.

Tyler dug five holes, and one by one he slowly pulled out each frog by its lifeless legs, dropping them in front of their respective holes for burial. My brother paused for a long moment and stared at the scene in front of him. Was he repenting for murdering one of God's creatures? Was he praying for them? Was he wondering what was cooking for lunch? No, it would turn out. His problem-solving wheels were clearly moving in his head. Tyler proceeded to flip each frog over on its back with its belly facing towards the sky and he began to pump on their stomach with his right thumb three times before moving to the next frog. He did this until all frogs had become victims twice over of his attempts at reviving them through CPR.

When I finally reached the scene, I saw before me five frogs that were squished so hard their eyes had popped out. It was a massacre. I scolded him again, lecturing him on how CPR only works if you're not already dead. We grabbed some twigs, made makeshift crosses that we stuck on the top of their graves to signify our Christian hope in the Resurrection and belief that death had been conquered.

The triangle rang from the deck signalling our call to grab lunch. We ran towards the cabin. My appetite was gone. My brother ate all his lunch really fast. The monster.

The lake was a place of many happy memories. For some reason, I recall this one the most.

LOVE IS IN THE AIR
AND IT SMELLS LIKE FARTS
~ For Sarah and Grant ~

There is a magnificent little jewel of an island in the outer rim of the Eastern Caribbean called St. Lucia. Geographically, it is shaped like a teardrop, one that likely fell from Heaven because it looks like paradise. St. Lucia is known as the beauty queen of the Caribbean. I was fortunate enough to find it unintentionally while googling cheap all-inclusive resorts, where a last minute low price sale was happening. I couldn't believe my wife and I could visit an all-inclusive 4.5 star resort for $800 each. There was no hesitation to book the trip since I'd only ever heard good things about St. Lucia.

St. Lucia has a lot of bang for your buck. It's a small island with a lot to see and do. It has crescent-shaped beaches with coarse volcanic sand (unless you visit the Sandal's 5-star resort down the road from ours, which has pristine soft white sand imported from Trinidad). There are quaint fishing villages with brightly coloured shanty houses and houses on stilts (because St. Lucia is very hilly, it's hard to build on levelled land). The island is one large rainforest that has coral reefs, waterfalls and geothermal hot springs known as the "Sulphur Springs" which are located in an active volcanic pit that spews mineral rich mud and sulphur. The therapeutic properties of these impressive natural hot spring baths are a significant attraction.

Towering above the St. Lucia skyline, best viewed from an ocean catamaran are the two iconic pyramid-shaped mountains that stand next to each other called the Gros Piton and Petit Piton.

In order to get to your resort, you have to drive in a tourist bus from the airport at the northern tip of the island, all the way to the southernmost tip, through winding roads that pass numerous banana plantations and palm trees.

Historically, St. Lucia was fought over by the French and the British in the 17th and 18th century no less than 14 times (it was occupied by the British seven times and by the French seven times). This is how it earned the nickname "Helen of the West Indies," referencing the beauty of the mythical Helen of Troy and those who fought for her. St. Lucia isn't a low-fare, low quality destination vacation where young adults come to party and trash the place. St. Lucia is for the serious romantics who seek the luxury of fine wining and dining, as well as the thrill of exhilarating adventure. Not far from our resort was the stunning Jade Mountain Resort, the location where a series finale for ABC's *The Bachelor* was filmed.

Our resort had marble flooring throughout the grounds, 45 acres of well-manicured lush tropical gardens, dim lighting and 4 separate buffet style restaurants that catered to different cuisines (Pan-Asian Fusion, Italian, Creole Seafood and traditional Caribbean beach barbeque).The resort also had cascading pools, with walk-up pool bars and a spa for massage and other treatments.

The St. Lucian staff were warm and incredibly outgoing, always smiling and going out of their way to talk with guests to make sure they felt comfortable. The entire place had an upper-class feel, and we felt out of place. Everywhere we walked, we inhaled hints of rum in the air. St. Lucia is known for making quality rum, and whether straight, mixed or in their desserts, people were drinking it from morning till night.

The resort was made for couples and every detail was designed with romance in mind. Even the dinners were eaten on a large dock with mood lighting that extended out into the bay so you could watch the sunset as you ate, drank wine and listened to live soft Caribbean steel drums serenading you while you stared into your lady's eyes.

For all the beauty the island had to offer, one thing that stood out like a sore thumb was the resort tour guide assigned to us on a couple of our excursions. Her name was Joy, and she actually came from the nearby Bahamas a few years prior. She accompanied my wife and I and four other couples to a four hour hike up the Gros Piton mountain and a tour of the sulphur springs in the world's only drive-in volcano.

Joy was this saucy, outspoken Caribbean woman with a large afro that was so spherical it had its own orbit. She'd strut around the resort like she didn't care what people thought of her. And as the trip went on, it would become quite apparent that she didn't mind how people perceived her. She did what she wanted.

On our first night there, Joy made fun of me while my wife and I were eating dinner on the dock. It was a fancy dinner and she happened to be nearby chatting to the wait staff and servers while we were ordering our food. She was within earshot of Hannah and I and overheard that I ordered an apple juice. She and the waiter broke into laughter because Hannah ordered a glass of wine, and me, an apple juice. They didn't know I'm allergic to wine and beer, and I wasn't feeling rum that evening (since I had way too much rum throughout the day already). I tried explaining that some people have an allergy to wine and beer, but they weren't hearing it. So, for the rest of the trip, anytime she'd see me on the resort she'd call me "Apple Juice" because I wasn't romantic enough to drink wine with my wife, in this beautiful part of the world. They even delivered my apple juice to me in a wine glass, to drive their joke home.

On one of the tours up to the Gros Piton mountain, Joy told us that she grew up in the Bahamas, a three-hour boat ride from St. Lucia. A few years ago, she was about to celebrate her wedding day with her husband-to-be and got cold feet at the last minute. She was on her way to the ceremony, had a panic attack and decided she couldn't go through with the commitment. Instead, she drove to one of the dockyards and took a one-way ferry over to St. Lucia. She took no belongings, told no one what she was doing, boarded the boat and never looked back. Joy said she'd been working on resorts in St. Lucia ever since and then went into a long spiel about how you don't need a partner to make you happy. In fact, getting married was a sure way to being miserable, she said.

My wife, and the other four couples weren't sure how to respond to her story, so we just continued on our way up the mountain. The Gros Piton is a strenuous two hour hike to the top. It's moderately easy to climb, but it's heavy on the body because as you climb higher the humidity restricts your ability to breathe. It doesn't feel like you're climbing a typical mountain, because it's completely covered in rainforest. It's more like trekking through a jungle where you see an obscene amount of tropical birds.

Half-way up, we encountered a massive mango tree. Joy told us it was over 300 years old. We marvelled at it and the concept that a tree could grow so old. Joy remarked, "Yeah, that's another reason it's not worth having a partner. They won't even make it to a third of the age of that tree before they die and leave you with nothing." You could see a few of the people raise their eyebrows as they listened to Joy. No one was too sure what to make of this cynical spinster who boldly contrasted this lover's paradise. As we continued towards the top, the views of the island inlets, turquoise water and colours of the small fishing villages nestled near the shores were stunning.

Instant peace washed over my body as I took in the scenery, until Joy opened her mouth, "We're almost at the top everyone, good work. That spot over there is where a tourist died last year. He was in his 50's, visiting with his wife and did this exact tour. At around this point, he stopped breathing and just collapsed, leaving his wife behind. You can't get medical teams up here, so they had to fly a helicopter up to evacuate him. Just in case that happens to you, take a few good looks at your partner here on this beautiful backdrop. I'll even use your camera to take a picture of you, in case you need one to remember the love you thought you had one day."

Some of us laughed at her comment, but we were mostly perplexed at the absurdity of this woman. Any tour company in North America would have fired her for making comments like that. In my head I was thinking, *I wonder if the resort realizes that this is the lady they hired to take couples who are in love on excursions around the island? Or maybe she is the only tour guide they could find that would willingly hike this thing with couples in high humidity?*

We made our way down, enjoying the view all over again, knees aching from taking the brunt of the impact with each step we'd take. Most of us had to ask for a few breaks on the way down. Joy made another comment as we waited for one hiker to catch their breath, "That's another thing I had to consider when I left my husband at the altar. One day his body will start falling apart. Do I really need that kind of burden to bear on my life as I get older?" People were too out of breath to even acknowledge or comment on what Joy had said. I also noticed that while our group was drenched in sweat, she didn't seem to perspire at all.

We got back to our resort later that evening, and feasted on some phenomenal Creole food, enjoying the grounds, sipping on fine rum while enjoying the sunset as we sat on the beach. We laughed about our tour guide and how ridiculous she sounded. I felt bad for her. It bothered me that she could live and work in a place so beautiful as St. Lucia and have such a negative outlook on love and life.

The next day, we were back at the tour circuit. This time, Joy took us to see the Sulphur Springs, which was a formerly active dome volcano that had a major eruption 40,000 years ago. It had a minor eruption in 1780, where the volcano dome collapsed, creating the Sulphur Springs you see today. The springs are massive craters filled with bubbling gravy-like ash that give off steam on the hill as you ascend it. If you pay a little extra, you can immerse your whole body in the mineral rich mud baths, which are really great for your skin. They serve you amazing food and drinks as you sit in the mud and enjoy the beautiful sights of the lush rainforest around you. The only problem is, because of the sulphur, the entire area smells like farts.

As we approached the main mud baths, Joy chimed in with a dry voice, "Welcome to the Sulphur Springs, St. Lucia's famous volcano. It smells terrible and reminds me that having a husband would mean I'd have to put up with that smell for the rest of my life. No thanks! I already have to smell this once a week, and that's enough." The couples laughed because it was less offensive than the other comments we'd heard her make the day prior. Nobody could tell if Joy was genuinely miserable or just putting on a show to make us do a double-take. I wouldn't find out until the very end of our trip.

On our last night at the resort, I went for a late night walk around the tropical gardens to take in the unique plants and flowers that were lit up with dimmed garden lights. The environment was serene and every few feet I'd see a gecko run across the path. I walked all the way to the front of the resort, where the gated entrance was. I could see a car pull up to the gate, and I noticed Joy walking towards it. A man and child hopped out of the car, and she ran towards them giving them both an affectionate hug and kiss. She got in the car and drove away.

The next morning, as we packed our things to get ready for the bumpy coach back to the airport, I ran into Joy at the breakfast buffet. I said, "Hey Joy, I went for a little stroll last night and saw you hugging what appeared to be a man you loved. You wouldn't happen to have been lying to us all week, were you?" With a bashful smile, she winked at me and explained that she puts on this cynical persona as a way to force couples to reflect on their love and cherish what they have. Then she said some words I'll never forget: "Love and the beauty that comes with it are worth fighting for, even when things are hard. Beauty and commitment come with suffering. If you aren't ready to suffer, you aren't ready for love." I knew Joy was a tour guide, but I had no idea she was a philosopher too.

Joy opened her backpack that she carried around with her and pulled out a little cloth baggie and said, "Here's a bag of dark roasted St. Lucian coffee beans from near the volcano. Take it home, make your wife a cup of coffee back in Canada and reflect on the beauty of this place and why you love each other." She sounded a bit like Jesus at the Last Supper. "Deal, I said," thankful for the kind gesture. I then reached into my black backpack and pulled out an apple juice box I had stolen from the buffet table an hour earlier.

"Here Joy, I want you to have this. Go share this apple juice with your husband and remember me and all the other people in the world that are allergic to wine and beer." She looked back at me with a gaze that questioned whether I was right in the head. I smiled and then swiped another two juice boxes from the buffet table after I made sure she had walked away. The bus ride back to the airport was long, hot and bumpy and I knew I'd be thirsty.

While Joy's approach was unorthodox, I admire her resolve to lead others to contemplate and cherish their love (I also admire her ability to stay in character the whole time). As it turns out, even when love smells like farts, it's utterly and unequivocally worth it.

TRACK IN THE USSR
~ For Naomi S. ~

I get that airplanes are faster and more efficient, but I think some of the best travelling is done when you have no other choice but to go slow. I've ridden trains in most of the nations I've been to, and you might think trains are the same wherever you go, but it just ain't true. If you want to get a good snapshot of a nation's culture, ride one of their trains.

By far, the most unique train experience I ever had was travelling from Moscow, Russia to Kiev, Ukraine in the summer of 2003. Once you factor in all the stops you make in towns and villages along the way, it ends up being a nine hour trip. I was expecting my train to look like the one in the 007 movie *From Russia with Love*. In the Bond movies, everyone wore classy suits and fancy dresses, had their own private carriage and ate elegant three course meals delivered to their door on a cart by a butler. The train in *FRWL* is the infamous Orient Express which, in real life, doesn't travel through Russia at all. The Orient Express is synonymous with luxury and intrigue, which is the complete opposite of the old Soviet passenger train I boarded. When I realized I wasn't going to be travelling for nine hours in luxury, I knew I'd be in for a long ride.

If you are as inexperienced about Russian rail travel as I was, allow me to indulge you in what such a train ride looks like.

Upon first boarding a Russian train, there are many things that meet the eye. First, the layout is all open-plan carriages with drop down beds and no private doors. The bunks, separated by a window, serve as both seat and bed, with a little side table to hold your beverages. A single train carriage can have forty-five other passengers, basically a tin of sardines. Everyone on the train looks like they need a nap or just woke up from one.

The open bunks are a little unnerving at first because you don't know who is sleeping below or across from you, and everyone looks angry with an air of melancholy surrounding them. That's a Russian thing though, something I never realized until our translator explained it to me. In the West, to show friendliness, we tend to acknowledge people with a smile or greeting. In Russia though, there's this old proverb that says, *"Smiling without a reason is a sign of being an idiot."* It's not that you can't ever smile, it just means that smiles are usually reserved for those you share close relationships with. It's why the Russians always make for good "bad guys" in the movies.

Another fun fact about Russian trains is that they are way too hot in the summer. This leaves the passengers with two options: open a window or take off most of your clothes. Many of the guys on the train end up shirtless and in their underwear, and nobody cares. Comfort comes before decency, and decency on the train is relative to a Russian.

There is a designated food car on the train, but it's often overpriced so passengers are way more likely to bring their own food or buy it from the merchants who come up to the bunk windows when the train is stopped. These merchants are usually old Russian ladies (babushkas), wearing flowery dresses and head scarfs, selling boiled eggs, bread and smoked fish. People in the carriage will stick their hands out the window to give the babushkas a few rubles in exchange for the food. After you make the trade, the babushka will kiss your hand three times (for the Father, Son and Spirit) as a way to say thanks.

Then there are the smells. A heavy combination of hot egg, fish, boiled potatoes and dill pickles are mingled with body odour that can get pretty rough, especially as people start shedding more clothing. It's a Russian tradition to share things, though, and the train ends up looking like a marketplace bazaar as passengers share food, talk loudly, laugh louder and occasionally start playing instruments.

During my trip, I had one of the top bunks and I spent a lot of time observing the comings and goings of everyone around me from that vantage point. At one point in the journey, someone a few beds down began to sing the entirety of the Russian folk song *Kalinka*, with others in the car joined in. Part way through, someone at the other end of the car busted out their violin to accompany the song. When they finished, people clapped throughout the carriage. Songs would start and stop throughout the journey by different people and different instruments, reminding me of duelling banjos.

The highlight of the ride was a group of eight people in my bunking area who began a game of Monopoly (the Russian version) and played it for a significant portion of the ride. They offered to have me play, but I couldn't understand their board so I opted to watch the game from my bunk where I had an aerial view of all the action. Monopoly is the epitome of capitalism, and I believe the game was banned in Russia until relatively recently for that reason.

The game began with much civility as people slowly bought up properties and railroads. Hard-boiled eggs, vodka and smoked meat were being shared amongst the players, and there were four people crammed to a seat on either side of the board game.

Monopoly brings out the worst in people, regardless of what country you play it in. If you've ever played it, you'll be acutely aware that when one player begins to get the upper hand, it's usually a slow grinding away at the rest of the participants as they slip into bankruptcy, hopelessness and despair. I've witnessed friendships and marriages almost fall apart on account of a Monopoly game gone south.

I witnessed the gamut of emotions during this particular game of Monopoly. Sasha, one of the men who shared my bunking area, had a bad case of dice luck, and only managed to own the more pathetic Russian equivalent properties of Baltic and Mediterranean Avenue. Eventually, Sasha managed to get two hotels up, due to the generosity and pity of the others who felt bad and handed him the money to do so. Despite his two properties, people kept managing to roll past them and each time they did, he would slam his fists down in a rage, understandably. You could see some tears welling up in his eyes as he slowly realized he would not be able to pass "GO" and collect $200 for much longer. Some of the participants let out a maniacal laugh each time Sasha rolled and landed on someone else's hotel. They also took pity on him though, offering to give him cash just to stay alive for one more turn. This just seemed to make Sasha angrier, though.

Igor, one of the other players who came from another cabin, was wearing no shirt and was one of the sweatier of the bunch. He leaned over to open the window because it became too hot. When he did so, his belly grazed the board, knocking it and everyone's Monopoly money to the floor. Arguments ensued over how to correctly re-administer the money because nobody could remember how much they had, and if they did, it became debated by someone else. Eventually, they agreed to divvy up the money evenly between them because nobody could see a fairer option, which, it turns out, is a very socialist approach to Monopoly. They even debated over where their metal game pieces were located on the board. Sasha, of course, tried his very best to argue that he was in jail, obviously. At that point in the game, jail was the safest place for him. He'd be homeless soon, and he knew it.

As the game dragged on, people began losing to a player named Julia who owned most of the properties. That's when the haggling started as the Russians endeavoured to "make the board more fair," again, missing the point of the game. Sasha, on the brink of annihilation, made a deal with Julia so that he could avoid having to pay her fees. They negotiated about it in Russian for a while, and then he walked off to another part of the train, coming back five minutes later with a large jar of honey, harvested from his own bee farm in Ukraine. Based on the look of despair on his face you'd think his net worth was that jar. He handed her the honey and sat down, looking like he'd just sold his soul only to live out a miserable existence.

It was Sasha's turn to roll, and he managed to land on one of Igor's hotels which instantly bankrupted him. The other seven players erupted in laughter because the bartering of honey for rent forgiveness he had done moments earlier lulled him into a false sense of security. Now he had no money, no property, and no honey. In shock, he began to argue passionately in Russian. I'm not sure what he said, but chunks of hard-boiled egg were spraying out of his mouth and onto the board before he stormed off. He was one mad Russian.

Julia decided to end the game by calling a draw because nobody was having fun anymore. She was happy, obviously, but not at the expense of seeing everyone else so frustrated. Eventually, Sasha came back, and they shared the honey amongst themselves with fresh bread and butter, renewing their friendship once again. As they critiqued the game over food and drink, their smiles and laughter came back and all animosity was seemingly forgiven. Julia even made sandwiches for the others as her way of apologizing for becoming a property tycoon.

In the end, the game of Monopoly ended up violating the Russian values for giving and sharing to those in need. Maybe such conflict wouldn't have occurred if they were playing a socialist version of Monopoly? I mean, it might be far less complicated to have a board game where the State provides you with a fixed income where a portion of your earnings covers your basic needs and you are not allowed to profit off of your neighbours, even if that would seem mutually advantageous. You couldn't sell property, because the State already owns it and if you passed GO to collect $200, you'd have to drop it right back in the middle of the board for the Kremlin to use to cover military expenditures. Nobody could be a winner, meaning everyone would be a winner, surely? I have no idea why Hasbro hasn't run with this concept yet...

The collapse of the game, much like their Soviet Union, led them all back to enjoying each other's company. We all partook of Sasha's honey, Julia's bread and black tea (with tons of sugar, as is custom). Before people would head back to their bunk beds, Sasha shared a Russian proverb that summed up our train journey perfectly: *"It's better to have a hundred friends than a hundred rubles."* I'm thankful I ended up in this third class style train, riding with this sweaty bunch and getting the chance to experience their warm (too warm) hospitality. A first-class train like the Orient Express would have had better food, sure, but often the food's only as good as the company. And, as we've established, as long as the company doesn't have a monopoly.

GOTTA CATCH 'EM ALL!
~For Kathleen~

When I was nine years old, I asked my parents if I could have a pet hamster. They had denied the request for several years prior, deferring it to one day when I could show more responsibility. The day came, and my father gave in to my request, allowing me to purchase my first hamster with the condition that I name it after him.

So, he drove me down to the local pet store, where I settled on a short-haired golden hamster from Syria. His name was Dan, and he was the best pet I ever had. Dan lived for four years, much longer than the average hamster lifespan. His long life can be attributed to the love and care I had for him. When he passed away, from old age, I buried him in a red and green Operation Christmas Child shoebox, in our backyard. We had some of these boxes left over from all the care packages we had made at church the previous Christmas. It's a good thing he didn't die near Christmas time though, otherwise, he could have easily been shipped out to a child for the holidays. That would have been a real tragedy.

I fed Dan well and provided him with a three story cage with luxurious amenities such as a plastic wheel for marathon running, a mushroom hut to sleep in, and a variety of clear plastic tubes to crawl through. At one point, buying the tubes got a little out of hand and my brother and I created "Tube City," a labyrinth of tunnels that ran throughout the basement. Tube City provided Dan with the adventure most hamsters in captivity only dream of. Dan wasn't just alive, he was living his best life.

In their natural habitat, the Syrian desert, hamsters are expert tunnellers and take great pleasure in digging through sand, specifically. Digging and rolling their bodies through the sand is how they clean dirt from their soft fur. In the summer, I would make a habit of taking Dan to the park that our house backed onto. This park had a treehouse, some monkey bars, a few classic swings and a large yellow slide with a hump in the middle that you could get serious air on if you wore sweatpants. Just off to the side of the park, was a large square sandbox for children to play in with a couple of benches on either side where parents would watch their little ones.

On days when the sandbox was empty, I would bring Dan to it so he could have the whole thing to himself. As soon as I put him in the sandbox, his wild instincts would kick in and he'd become a little crazy, digging really fast, rolling his body back and forth in a cloud of dust, and then eventually tunnelling. He followed a strict pattern, which was to dig with his front paws, kick the excess sand out of the hole behind him with his back paws, and then he'd poke his head out of the top to look at you right before going back to digging. Dan had a blast in that sandbox; whenever I'd try to pick him up to bring him home, he'd try to run away, like a kid who doesn't want to come home from a theme park.

My eight year old brother Tyler, who looked up to me as a role model and shining example of how to responsibly care for an animal, made a second request to my parents to purchase his own hamster. His first request happened three months earlier, which my parents agreed to on the condition that he could take care of it. A week after getting his hamster, he left the cage open and his hamster took off. We found him several days later. He had fallen into the basement sump pump. He didn't survive.

This experience traumatized my brother. He had been looking forward to owning his own hamster for almost a year. Tyler put much care into preparing for his very own hamster: his cage looked awesome and his food and accessories were all ready to provide the same kind of love and care that Dan had received. Tyler was devastated, shedding many tears, my mother consoling him in his bedroom as he grieved. My parents were tempted to go out and buy him another one, but they needed him to understand how much of a responsibility it is to take care of animals, lest something tragic like this happen again.

His conditions for purchasing a new hamster were that for the next three months, he would have to make his bed every morning, clean his room and help load the dishwasher. If he could maintain this, they would let him have his own hamster again. Well, the three month mark came and he was successful. Tyler was motivated, and he even made sure his cage had a special latch on the door that ensured it could never be left open once the hamster was inside. My parents were proud of him. I was proud of him. No longer would Tyler live in the shadow of his responsible older brother. He was ready to break out of that limiting shell, spread his wings and fly into his own destiny as a pet owner.

Like a proud parent, Tyler brought Junior home and gently placed him in his cage. A week went by, and no accidents happened. Junior remained in his cage, and Tyler was feeding him and handling him with great care. Tyler really took ownership of this latest hamster and we could all tell that something had changed internally for him.

One afternoon, my brother asked if he could take Junior to the sandpit and let him roam free, as I had done for Dan so many times before. I agreed to go with him and sit on the bench next to the pit so I could "supervise" while playing my Gameboy pocket. Pokémon was the new thing, and I was on a mission to "catch 'em all."

It was a sunny day, as it often is during the summer in Manitoba. Kids were at the park enjoying themselves. Tyler was eating a popsicle while his hamster burrowed into the sand happily. I was catching Pokémon. We were doing what kids are supposed to be doing. I asked Tyler how his hamster was doing. He smiled and said, "Good!" as he sat two feet away from it, being careful not to drip popsicle juice on the critter. The joy of his prized hamster was all over his face.

As I was focused on my Pokémon video game, I noticed a shadow pass over my head, blocking the sun for a moment. I figured it must have been a lone cloud passing by and I didn't mind the temporary shade since it allowed me to see my screen much better. I then noticed the shadow reappear, this time getting smaller and smaller. I looked up to the sky to see a bird of prey circling high above us before dropping down like a stealth bomber.

Everything happened so fast, there was no time to act. The bird nose dived right into the pit where its talons grabbed Tyler's hamster. Before either of us could react, it flew away with Junior in its clutches, but not before it circled above us, hamster in tow, as if to taunt us.

As we watched Tyler's pet fly away, neither of us could say or do anything. That moment felt like eternal helplessness. His soul was crushed, and so was his hamster (man, that bird had a serious grip). That was the last day that Tyler owned a hamster. He would never buy another one (or any mammal, for that matter).

He owns fish now.

TERRIBLE TERRY
FROM CANADA POST
~ For David M. ~

We went on a holiday to Cuba to celebrate the completion of my B.A. We were student poor, and found a cheap all-inclusive vacation for seven days in Holguin, Cuba. Our particular resort had tourists mostly from Ontario and Quebec. Unlike the rest of the Caribbean, you don't see too many Americans in Cuba.

The resort was far from any major city and felt incredibly isolated. After landing in Holguin with our Sunwing.ca plane, we took a 1.5 hour bus ride to the resort. That bus ride drove us through some very poor areas with a lot of character and friendly faces. The streets were a mix of red dirt and gravel, and the houses were mostly made of concrete with no glass windows, and instead, wood or metal shutters.

We had a more modern coach bus, but if there are cars on the road (and there aren't a lot), they are usually from the 1950s, the last time Americans imported cars to Cuba. Car ownership in Cuba is low, as a result of this. Most Cubans take the bus, walk or use motorcycles. Hitchhiking is commonplace.

Cuba has quite the contrasts. People generally make the equivalent of $25 - $45 a month in public jobs and can make more in the tourism industry. Doctors, engineers, lawyers, and teachers all make similar wages. They have a 99.8% literacy rate though and have some of the finest doctors. Also, Cubans receive a large amount of support from their government in the form of healthcare, education and food subsidies, while having low costs of living. When visiting, the Cubans we met said that life there is not luxurious, but it is comfortable. If you had to be poor anywhere, Cuba would be one of the best places to do it.

Not only that, but Cuba is just charmingly beautiful. I've never seen sand so pristinely white and waters so blue. The people in Cuba seem to take things in stride. They appear to have really adopted the phrase "live beneath your means," mostly due to economic necessity. From renovating houses to fixing cars and boats, you can see Cuban ingenuity all over the place. They do the best they can with what they have and seem to shrug when things don't go as efficiently as they could, just getting on with it. People don't seem too phased by adhering to strict schedules and place a large emphasis on relationships.

Our resort was very basic. It had some villas facing the ocean, a central pool, a large buffet style hall for meals and an evening lounge for dancing that was positioned right near the beach. The lounge was self-contained, had a bar and walls made of mirrors to multiply the coloured lighting while people danced to Cuban music, which is really a combination of rhumba and salsa with some Spanish fusion amongst other influences. Cuban culture is a dancing culture.

Sometimes I wish that certain scenes in life had background music playing, to add effect. At our Cuban resort, we had it. There was a trio of male performers that would stand near the beach bar singing all day. Specifically, they sang a catchy song called *Gaujira Gauntanamera* more frequently than any other song. They were older men who all had a role. The tallest man played the Spanish guitar and only had one eye. The other two guys played small portable bongo drums and shook maracas. All three of them sang along.

Every morning, we would eat our breakfast in the buffet, always the same thing, and always lacking in flavour (Cuban resorts are not known for their food). After breakfast, you could head over to the beach bar for your morning coffee, where Juan would serve you. Juan, a nuclear physicist and engineer trained in Moscow, chose to work as a bartender on the resort because it paid quite a bit more than being a nuclear physicist in Cuba. It's kind of the same thing though because instead of mixing radioactive isotopes, he was now making elaborate alcoholic concoctions for the tourists.

Spanish coffee is coffee with shots of rum, to start the morning off right. It helps you forget how terrible the breakfast was and relax quickly. It would be a couple of days into our stay at this resort before I realized they were putting alcohol in my coffee each morning. I figured a Spanish coffee was just a type of bean roast, though I had wondered why I looked forward to my morning coffee more than usual in Cuba.

As we sat at the coffee bar talking to Juan while enjoying the sun and ocean air, an older gentleman strolled up to the bar to order his own Spanish coffee. It would turn out that he was not in fact, a gentleman at all. His name was Terry, and he worked for Canada Post, as he would introduce himself to everyone, even to the Cubans who had no idea what Canada Post was. Juan told me that Terry was a frequent visitor to this resort, coming every year. He earned the nickname "Terrible Terry" amongst the resort staff because of his obnoxious behaviour and inability to control his drinking. They didn't want him at the resort, but they couldn't afford to turn away business.

Terry was usually drunk by 9 am and was often dancing even when music wasn't playing. He'd stand near the three Cuban singers when they were performing and would dance, terribly. Then he'd wander off to the beach for most of the day and show up again in the evening for dinner at the buffet restaurant before meandering over to the dance lounge.

Terry was rude, demanding, and narcissistic. He would complain about service and nit-pick at the resort workers for things of little consequence to a rational human being. Terry was a loose cannon that nobody reigned in.

Terry travelled with his girlfriend, and everyone witnessed them break up and get back together numerous times in a single day. Their relationship was very dramatic and it was bizarre to watch their drastic ups and downs. They'd sit at different tables for lunch in the buffet hall because they were upset with one another, and then be laughing together and holding hands at the same table come dinner time.

One morning when we were drinking our Spanish coffees at the bar with Juan, Terry was already on his second drink and looking sloshed. Like a hippo ballerina, Terry did an undignified twirl towards Juan and asked him to translate a request to the Cuban singers. Juan spoke to the Cuban singers, coming back to Terry and said, "Sorry, they prefer to stay by the bar to perform."

Terry had asked if the three Cuban singers would follow him throughout the day, performing background music wherever Terry went. They turned him down. Terry, angered by this, launched into a rant about how people don't treat Canada Post employees with the respect they deserve anymore. He walked away in a tuff, coming back 10 minutes later with $100 cash. He waved the bills in the faces of the singers and told Juan he would give them the stack if they'd reconsider, which they did. But, they didn't look like they were happy about it. Begrudgingly, they took Terry's money and followed him around the resort playing *Guantanamera* with the guitar, bongos and maracas for the rest of the day.

Terry would go to the beach for a swim and the singers would go to the beach with him and serenade him from the sand (usually under a shady palm tree). Terry would go to his bathroom in his villa, the trio would play outside his villa door while they waited for him. Terry would go to the buffet, and they'd stand near his table, singing away. Terry thought it was great, everyone else thought it was rude and insulting to the Cuban singers.

Later that evening, Terry was seen wandering over to the dance lounge near the beach as the music and dance were kicking off. You could see his white hair, red sunburnt skin and unbuttoned Hawaiian shirt from a mile away. Terry was alone, his girlfriend was back in their room having locked Terry out, obviously having just had another fight. He was heavily intoxicated as he stumbled towards the dance lounge.

As the night went on, Terry took a seat at one of the raised circular tables off to the side of the dance floor. He sat next to the mirrored wall and began to argue with the man in front of him, who also happened to be himself. Indignant, Terry began shouting at his reflection. Being the spectacle that he was, the three Cuban singers took it upon themselves to get a little redemption from their earlier humiliation. They came alongside Terry and began to serenade him, keeping their end of the bargain to follow him around and play.

Other tourists on the dance floor clapped along with the music, forming a semi-circle around Terry. We're not sure if it was what the other guy was saying, or if the crowd set him off, but Terry began to throw fists at himself in the mirror, breaking it and cutting his hand. As blood ran down his hands, urine streamed down his legs. His incontinence led to several tourists carrying him out of the dance lounge and back out to his villa, only Terry was too drunk to walk or make his way into his room.

Terry slept the night on the veranda, hands and feet tied neatly to the railing for his own safety, so he wouldn't fall into the resort pool. He was a postman by day and a perfectly wrapped parcel by night. Terry was half asleep and one side of his pant leg was wet from urine. He was one package nobody wanted to sign for, except for the resort security guards who took him away and banned him from ever returning.

The next day, a feast was held to celebrate Terrible Terry's banishment from the resort. A wealthy Canadian tourist paid for a massive pig to be roasted on the beach that evening, inviting the resort workers and their families to feast. He served the workers to honour them for their service, trying to convey a better Canadian way. He also apologetically paid the three Cuban singers $300 as reparations for Terry's actions.

Terry's girlfriend stayed the rest of the week at the resort without him. Smart girl.

MERRY CHRISTMAS JEFFREY
~ For Rachael & Wayne ~

It was 5:30 am on Christmas Eve. It was still very dark outside, the only light was from the white glow of the street lamps. It was -25 degrees Celsius, the air was crisp and dry and we could see trails of steam rising from the street sewer grates. My wife and I were wearing our winter clothing, as we stood there shivering, waiting for our bus to pick us up.

We walked to the stop from our little flat and grabbed a hot cup of coffee with the dual purpose of helping us wake up and keeping us warm while we waited. People don't realize it, but winters in Korea are extremely cold. Dry Siberian winter air blows from Northern Russia and down through the entire Korean peninsula. This would be the first Christmas that my wife and I would spend away from our families, and we wanted it to be memorable. So, we paid for a tour of the demilitarized zone (DMZ) on the border of North and South Korea.

You hear a lot about the DMZ and North Korea in Western media, and while the average South Korean doesn't give much thought to North Korea (or take their threat seriously), most foreigners find it an intriguing enigma. Prior to our trip to the DMZ, Hannah did a little bit of volunteer work teaching English at the U.N. defection site for North Koreans who had recently arrived in South Korea. North Korean defectors stay in a resettlement center in Seoul for several months, where they are gradually eased into life in the

South (taught about bank accounts, employment, medical attention, South Korean customs, and even a little bit of English). Hannah's experience working with defectors made the trip very real to us, being able to put faces to this so-called "monster to the north".

The Korean War began in 1950, shortly after World War II, when the military forces of North Korea crossed the 38th parallel into South Korea. Having recently gained independence from Japanese colonial rule, Korea was at war with itself. The geopolitical influences of ideology and empire could not be escaped. The North would be supported by the Soviets and China, while the South would be supported by democratic nations (the U.S. and others).

More than five million people would die during the war that lasted three years. In 1953, an armistice was signed to end active fighting between the North and South, but the war was never officially declared over. The DMZ is the literal buffer zone between North and South and is known as the most heavily protected and reinforced border in the world. A lovely place to spend Christmas.

The DMZ stretches from coast to coast on the peninsula and is about 2.5 miles wide. That strip of land has been untouched by humans since the armistice was signed, over six decades ago. The DMZ is fortified with tall, barbed-wire fences, scattered with land mines and guarded by each country's military.

Every now and then, you will hear of gunfight skirmishes that break out inside the DMZ between the North Korean People's Army (KPA) and the Republic of South Korea (ROK) soldiers. The cause for this is usually someone trying to defect from the North into the South. For this reason, the DMZ can be very dangerous, especially if this happens while a civilian tour is happening (like the one we were about to do). In fact, two weeks prior to our tour, a defector ran across the "line" and a gunfight broke out.

Before entering the DMZ, the tour bus stops at a building where you are briefed by military personnel and made to sign a form stating that you're aware of the risks, should you be harmed or killed as a result of being in the DMZ. After all legalities are complete, you get back on the bus and head to the Joint Security Area (JSA).

The JSA is what most people think of when they hear about the DMZ. It's the only part of the area where North and South Korean soldiers stand face to face. A line in the ground divides North from South and three small blue buildings sit directly along that line.

These buildings are where diplomatic negotiations happen between the North and South. One door lets you in from the North, and another from the South, acting as literal doors to each country.

On the South side, these buildings are guarded by ROK soldiers and American soldiers. They stand facing the North, with half of their bodies covered by the blue building and the other half exposed to the North, a stance meant to intimidate and show that they are ready in case hostilities kick off. It's all very heavy and tense in the atmosphere there, for good reason.

That morning, a heavy fog blanketed the area, and the trees, lifeless from the frosty weather made the experience all the more ominous. Everything appeared to be one shade of grey, ironic I thought, since wherever you look in the DMZ, all you see are the competing contrasts between North and South.

Once we arrived in the JSA, we were taken to a room where we were briefed on the rules for proper conduct by the soldiers. One soldier, who doubled as a tour guide, was assigned to each group.

Well, the soldier they assigned to us just so happened to be a young man from the U.S. named Jeffrey. Jeffrey had a high pitched squeaky voice, making us question if puberty was a recent event for him. With gangly arms and a frail physique, Jeffrey's military uniform hung off his shoulders like a tent, further amplifying his recent (if not ongoing) journey into manhood. Jeffrey was also newly stationed in Korea, and it showed.

Our young soldier friend was armed, and his job was to address the tourists in the room on the rules prior to leading us on the tour. No revealing/inappropriate clothing. You must NEVER make rude gestures towards the KPA soldiers. Doing so could escalate tensions, but also get you physically "dealt with" by ROK soldiers whose life you might also put at risk. You must have your identification badge hanging around your neck at all times. If you decide to jokingly run across the line, you might never return. Easy rules to follow.

While the rules were simple enough, there was something particularly perplexing: Jeffrey was nervous, very nervous. When he addressed us, he read off of a sheet and didn't look up from it once. He appeared rushed and his breathing wasn't controlled. He stuttered and stumbled through many of his words, his face getting noticeably redder with each mistake he made. He was also perspiring, quite heavily. It couldn't have been the weather, either, because it was freezing out.

We couldn't tell if Jeffrey was just socially anxious or terrified by being in the DMZ, himself.

Either way, he was making the rest of the tourists nervous. The thought that was continually running through my mind was, *Great, if a defector decides to run and guns start popping off, Jeffrey is supposed to protect us?*

As we continued our tour, Jeffrey took us into a museum room that displayed articles of clothing and weapons from previous fatal skirmishes between soldiers at the DMZ, where he nervously told us about their historical significance. Some of these relics were from the South, others from the North.

From there, Jeffrey took us into the 3rd infiltration tunnel that was discovered in 1978 by the South Koreans after a North Korean defector tipped them off about it. It went 240 feet deep underground and the North Koreans had tunnelled it as a way to invade Seoul with ground infantry. Jeffrey's voice quivered as he explained the history of the tunnel and the elaborate plans of the North to raid the South. The tunnel is actually quite creepy, and the tour takes you right to the spot where it would cross into the North, but it's been blocked off with barbed wire and a few physical barricades. On average, the North Korean people are smaller in stature than North Americans, so the tunnel felt especially claustrophobic since we had to crouch the whole time we were down there.

The next stop was going inside the blue buildings that share the divide between the borders. Once inside, you can move around freely, meaning, you are technically in North Korea when you step over the clearly marked line on the floor. The door to North Korea stands in front of you, but it is guarded by a ROK soldier with a third degree black belt in Tae Kwondo or Judo, and he is ready to knock you out if you get too close. ROK soldiers wear black shades to hide their eyes. Jeffrey would have benefited from a pair, to hide the fear in his eyes, but his crackling voice would have given him away.

Jeffrey became very agitated as we stood in front of the ROK soldier to take pictures with him. He kept notifying us about the time, and how we would have to leave the building soon. It was obvious that Jeffrey wanted to get out of that building as quickly as possible.

At the end of our walking tour, Jeffrey was supposed to escort us back to our bus to ensure our safety and wrap up the tour. As we began to approach our ride, the driver noticed us and put his keys in the ignition to start the engine. It made quite a loud backfiring noise which startled most of us for a moment before we realized it was the bus that made the loud bang.

But Jeffrey…. Jeffrey let out a yelp, and ran for cover behind a building near the bus, abandoning our tour group on the path, now exposed to the fake gunfire he clearly thought was real. The rest of us continued on, boarding the bus and looking back at Jeffrey as he cowered behind the building. He was obviously shaken, and not so good at hiding it.

We could all see him from the tinted bus windows as we took our seats. He stood with his back against the building wall and pulled out his radio, pretending to speak into it. He then walked away from us, not saying goodbye, likely embarrassed at what had just happened. He was supposed to do an attendance count on our bus but didn't. So, the bus driver just left.

Maybe it was a case of the new job jitters, or maybe it was a legitimate concern of being caught in a Korean crossfire. I'm not sure what he was so anxious about, but I hope Jeffrey was able to overcome his fears, and I hope had a great Christmas. I hope even more that the North never realizes that Jeffrey is the one guarding the South, otherwise they might get brave and realize they don't even need a tunnel.

SINGAPORE'S MOST WANTED
~ For Sean & Anne ~

I met my friend Sean while teaching in Korea and he shared a most unfortunate story with me that happened alongside my own experiences living in Asia. He recounted his experience while we sat at the local 7-11 patio drinking a quick beer after a particularly long and stressful day of teaching. I grew up in Winnipeg, Canada which is unofficially known as the 7-11 Slurpee capital of the world, so seeing 7-11's in Korea was a source of comfort for the occasional bouts of homesickness I'd experience.

Laughter, for me, is the best medicine for anything, so I feel I have a duty to share Sean's story as it was recounted to me in the hope that it will make you feel better about yourself in case you're having a crappy day.

I worked with a handful of English teachers that had come over from Canada, the U.S. and Britain. We worked long days teaching English to elementary and high school students after the kids had just completed a full-day of "regular" school, a practice that is common in Korea. The country places a very high value on education, so it is not uncommon for children to attend a variety of tutoring or private academies after they finish their day at 3 pm.

English teachers, specifically, are held in high regard because Korean's understand how English is in the international business arena, where Korea has become a powerhouse in the last 40 years. It follows then, that native English speakers coming to Korea are given an honoured welcome and a lot of incentives to remain there. Some of these incentives include free housing, significant holiday time and bonuses for extending teaching contracts.

Sean was a much liked teacher and was able to negotiate an extra month off at the end of his contract if he agreed to return for another year. He used this additional month to do some extended travelling in South East Asian nations close to Korea like Vietnam, Singapore, Thailand and China. He was a solo traveller and did these trips completely on his own, trying to maximize the most bang for his buck.

The first country on his itinerary was Singapore and he shared the following story (which I think was more of a confession) with me after he had consumed his second beer on the patio of 7-11.

He wanted to start his trip off right with a few relaxing days to unwind on one of Singapore's beaches before heading out to the airport where he'd fly to Vietnam to begin the more adventurous part of his vacation. After googling some low budget couch-surfing options, he found an Airbnb in the perfect neighbourhood. The ad said that for $10 a night he could sleep on the host's living room sofa. A bonus was that they would cook him two meals a day. There was a single name attached to the booking option and naturally, Sean assumed he'd be sharing the apartment with one other person.

When he arrived in Singapore, he hailed a taxi that drove him to a tall white apartment building that overlooked the beautiful beaches of Singapore. He tipped the driver, grabbed his bag and headed into the main entrance by following a charming stone path lined with tall palm trees.

He rode the elevator up to the tenth floor, knocked on the door and to his surprise, was greeted by an entire family. There was a husband, wife, two children and an elderly grandmother who all lived in this humble three bedroom apartment. The family spoke limited English and stared at him with reserved curiosity as they invited him in for dinner.

He was only staying for three nights before heading off to Vietnam; he ate his dinner with the family, put his bags in a closet and went to bed on the couch they prepared for him so he could get up early and head to the beach the next morning. The father told

Sean that their front door would always remain unlocked so that he could enter and exit as needed.

Singapore is one of the safest countries to visit in the world so this was not unusual to leave the door unlocked. Another thing about Singapore is that it has some of the world's strictest littering and cleanliness laws. Singapore is one of the only places in the world that has specific legislation against flushing public toilets or urinating in elevators. If caught leaving a toilet unflushed, you can expect to pay a hefty fine. Many Singaporean elevators are also equipped with Urine Detection Devices which, upon detecting the scent of urine, will set off an alarm and keep the doors closed until a police officer arrives. Breaking their cleanliness laws after first convictions can also land you jail time.

The first two days were relaxing and went as planned. He woke up, had a light breakfast with rice and vegetables and then ventured to the beach where he stayed all day until the sun went down. In the evenings, he would quietly return to the apartment and pass out on the comfy leather couch that had been assigned just to him. He barely saw the family he was staying with and when they did see each other, the family was very quiet and avoidant (perhaps the perfect hosts).

What a lot of people don't tell you when you're travelling to South East Asia though, is that it takes some time for a visitor's stomach to adjust to the different germs and bacteria that come with eating in a foreign land. For the first two days, Sean was seemingly unaffected. He'd had roughly six meals by now and wasn't feeling ill, probably due to the stomach of iron he developed from drinking so much Korean beer in the last twelve months. On his third night, however, the night before leaving for Vietnam, his body fell prey to a nasty bug. The kind that you hope and pray you'll never catch outside the comfort and familiarity of your own home.

It was the middle of the night and he had been sleeping for about two hours when he woke up on the couch drenched in sweat from head to toe. His skin was clammy and his hair looked like he had just gotten out of the shower, completely soaked. His stomach was experiencing intermittent searing pains and he came to the horrifying realization that he had lost complete control of his bowels while he had been sleeping. Sean had crapped his pants on the black leather couch of his Airbnb hosts. He sat there, delirious, half-awake and fully panicked with adrenaline rushing through his body while he laboured internally over how he should deal with the very literal mess on his hands.

The living room where he was sleeping was the focal point of the small apartment. To the left of the couch was the kitchen. Directly behind him was the shared bathroom that the whole house used, and to the right of that was a small hallway with three doors to the three bedrooms currently occupied with all the (hopefully) sleeping family members. In fact, two of the bedrooms had doors that were slightly open so they could potentially hear him if he made any loud noises.

In front of the couch were three large windows and a sliding glass door to the balcony where you could see a lovely view of the beach during the day. It was pitch black, though, and all he could see was the reflection of his shame ridden face.

A surge of fear filled Sean's body as he assessed his surroundings with his poor night vision and the growing realization he had few options for how to respond to the unfolding crisis in front of him. He managed to carry himself to the bathroom, quietly shut the door and cleaned himself up. He had a fresh pair of underwear, extra shorts to replace his pyjama pants, and a new t-shirt in the small luggage bag that was sitting in the closet near the couch.

The problem was that he was left with the need to dispose of his heavily soiled underwear and pants as well as the mess that was still on the black leather couch in the living room. "What am I supposed to do with my clothes?!" his mind raced. "I can't throw them in the garbage, because the family will know and it will smell. I can't put them in my bag because my bag stays beside the couch, and they will smell that too" he conversed with himself. He taught English but it was incredibly difficult for him to put words to the array of emotions he was experiencing as he tried to dig himself out of this hole.

Sean put his thoughts on pause, left his filthy clothes on the bathroom floor and decided to tackle the more immediate problem of what remained on the couch. Like a panther on the prowl, he turned off the bathroom light, quietly opened the door, and slowly made his way to the couch where he began to scrub it down as best as he could. Thankfully, it was a leather couch and not fabric. This took him way longer than it should have, because he was tippy-toeing from the bathroom to the couch, meticulously cleaning the mess with one toilet paper sheet at a time. He was successful though. He managed to clean up the mess and flush the evidence down the toilet, where it belonged in the first place. Not out of the woods yet, he just had to deal with his own soiled clothing sitting on the bathroom floor.

Needing a break, he took a seat on his freshly cleansed couch, contemplating what he should do. He looked out of the living room windows into the starry Singaporean sky from ten levels up, wishing he could just disappear into the darkness. In a moment of helpless desperation, Sean made a quick decision he strongly regrets to this day. Maybe it was his high fever, or maybe it was just a sense of hopelessness and fight or flight response his anxious body was in. We'll never know.

With reluctant determination, he walked from the balcony windows back to the bathroom and picked up his soiled underwear. He walked back to the balcony window. With his right hand, he scrunched his underwear and pyjama pants into a tight ball and gently used his left hand to unlock the latch, which he then pulled open ever so slowly to minimize noise.

He walked to the edge of the balcony and catapulted his clothing into the void in front of him. Relieved, he went back inside, washed his hands, and went back to sleep on the couch. It was a mission he was not proud to complete, but the crisis was averted.

The next morning, he woke up to the smell of breakfast being cooked by the wife and the kids setting the table. He got dressed, brushed his teeth and packed his bag in great anticipation to leave the apartment. As the family sat down to eat, he joined them. The breakfast table was quiet. Maybe it was his paranoia, or maybe it was his lingering fever, but Sean became increasingly paranoid that the family had secretly witnessed his shameful shenanigans. Anxiety whelmed up within him and it became too much for Sean to handle.

He promptly finished his food, pointed to his watch and mumbled something about an airplane and being late and how he had to leave right away to catch his taxi. He handed the family thirty dollars plus an extra twenty as a tip for their kindness and to soothe his guilty conscience. The husband and family bowed their heads in thanks and opened the door to see him out.

Sean breathed a sigh of relief as he pushed the elevator button down to the lobby. That could have gone much worse than it had. He could put this all behind him and really enjoy his vacation now with a fresh start. Vietnam would be a new beginning, but not without first making a quick stop to pick up some Imodium from the airport pharmacy.

His elevator reached the ground level, he wheeled his luggage bag out the lobby doors and could see his taxi out front waiting for him. As he was walking out the front doors on that beautiful stone path lined with palm trees, he could see his pyjama pants and dirty underwear directly in front of him hanging from a tree for all to see. Anyone and everyone who entered the building was now exposed to his soiled undergarments.

He broke into a quick jog towards the taxi, pretending he didn't notice, threw his bag in the back and high-tailed it out of there to the airport, head hanging low in shame, a stain on Singapore's Airbnb industry and now possibly on their "most wanted" list for breaking their strict littering and cleanliness laws.

YABBA DABBA DOO!
~ For Paul S. ~

I took my boys to the local park this evening to play on the playground for a couple of hours.

My wife was preparing for a difficult math test she would have to write later that night and needed silence. She is studying Medical Radiation Sciences at university and is required to pass a mandatory math class that has driven her to tears on more than one occasion. Math is the worst. I failed it in high school and have strategically made career decisions that would allow me to avoid math whenever possible. A high school teacher once told me, "When you look for a career one day, play to your strengths otherwise you'll be fighting an uphill battle most of your life and you'll be miserable." So, now I'm a therapist and talk about feelings instead of numbers, unless I happen to notice that you didn't pay the full session fee. Then, for a moment, I'm an expert at numbers.

My wife's request was that I take both of our boys, who are five and three, out of the house for two hours so she could study in peace and quiet. "No problem," I said,"I'll take the kids out for a burger and fries and then we'll hit up the playground. That should tire them out enough before bed." Bedtime is a bit of a nightmare at our house. You'd think that five years of the same bedtime routine every single night would make it easier for them to just accept the inevitable. But no, they have to resist it and make things difficult for me, every single night.

We live in Hamilton, Ontario, on top of the Niagara Escarpment, which is a huge, forested ridge known by the locals as "the mountain" and it's dotted with trails, waterfalls and trees of all kinds. It overlooks the rest of Hamilton and Lake Ontario and sits about 100m higher than the rest of the city. Parks in Hamilton tend to be pretty well maintained, often having decent playgrounds that include splash pads for the kids to use in the summer.We're fortunate to have access to these parks and local beauty.

When we go to the playground, my kids always ask to play a game they made up called "Zombie Chase." The way it works is, I am the zombie, and I have to chase them while they attempt to evade me. I have to make zombie gurgling noises while I chase them and walk like I'm a mummy. They find a lot of joy in this, and the only person that gets tired of it is me. They'd never have me stop if I didn't set a limit.

On this particular day, I chose to go to a park that we don't often visit. The park itself is quite generic. It has a couple sets of monkey bars, a central jungle gym island with ladders, spiral pipes for climbing and a few slides. The slides are those large thick plastic ones that look like they'll be a lot of fun, until you go down and get massive static electric shocks that traumatize children and adults alike. I think the designers intended that when creating the slides though, as a natural way to prevent too many children from using the slide at the same time. It's like a large bug zapper for children.

The surfacing of the playground is a thick bed of wood chips that provides some cushion to soften the blow if you fall down while running away from Zombie Dad. Park designers use the wood chips because they are effective for averting injuries and are less sensitive to extreme temperatures. The wood chips are made of cedar and actually provide quite a nice smell, but they are notorious for getting stuck in your shoes and socks. Half of the time spent at the playground is devoted to playing, while the other half is spent pulling rogue wood chips out of your shoes.

In the end, "Zombie Chase" ends up being less of a chase, and more of a start and stop game with long pauses for wood chip removal and calming the frustrated emotions of your kids who can't understand how the wood chips keep slipping in. What starts as a plan to tire my kids out, ends up exhausting me instead because my kids need help getting their shoes on and off, about forty times.

Needing a break, I told my kids to try and play on their own for a bit while I sat on a nearby bench that was damp from the moist October air.

I took a sip of my water bottle, reflecting on how out of shape I was and looked at my watch. I needed to kill two hours at the park and we had only been there for one. One more hour to go.

As I was sitting at the bench, observing my own kids and daydreaming about life, a father and his three kids approached the park from the adjacent street. This father would introduce himself to me as Mike.

Mike and his three kids looked like they had just escaped a fire, or had been living in a nearby bush. Mike's hair was unwashed and unkempt with cowlicks moving in a few different directions. He was wearing sweatpants with holes in various places and a faded white t-shirt that said "Kellogg's Corn Flakes" with a large green rooster on the front. I want to say that he was wearing his indoor clothes, but I got the feeling that Mike doesn't differentiate between indoor and outdoor clothing.

Mike was completely barefoot.

"Where are your shoes, I said?" with curiosity.

"Oh, I just live a few streets down the main road," he replied. Not really an explanation, I thought but nodded as if I understood his logic.

I could see the wood chips wedged between his toes as I glanced down at his feet, but he didn't seem to care. He had an extra-large red Tim Horton's coffee he was nursing as he sat on the bench, staring at the park with a glazed look of indifference in his eyes.

Both sets of kids were enjoying themselves until they got into an argument over who's turn it was to ride the spring rider, a seating component in the shape of an alligator with a spring placed into the ground. Once a kid sits on it, they can rock back and forth with a little bounce. Oodles of fun for about 10 seconds before you get bored and move on to something else. But, the universal laws of the playground state that if one kid is using one piece of playground equipment, the others must follow him and argue about having a turn, even if it's boring.

"Kids are just exhausting. They have no concept of sharing or taking turns," Mike said, without any prompting.

"Yeah, that's true," I laughed, in agreement.

"Did you have a tough day at work?" I asked.

Mike then explained to me that he had been laid off work since March due to the COVID-19 pandemic. He told me how his wife used to care for their children, but she went back to work as a nurse right around the time the pandemic broke out, leaving Mike to be a stay at home dad for the last seven months.

"You must be exhausted," I tried to validate.

"Bro, you have no idea. It's Kraft Dinner and hot dogs every day for dinner and they want my attention at every moment because they aren't allowed to hang out with their friends or go to school," Mike replied.

Just then, all of Mike's kids ran over to him, begging him to play with them on the climbing structure or chase them in a game of tag. Mike responded, "I told you guys, I'm too tired. Now, if you want to earn some treats, you have to go find forty pine cones and leave me alone here on the bench to rest." The kids seemed oddly excited by their father's instructions to find forty pinecones in the trees that lined the perimeter of the playground.

Mike reached his hand into one of his pant pockets and pulled out a white bottle that said "Flintstones Chewable Vitamins" on the cover. He unscrewed it and handed them each one chewable Flintstone character that they likely had no knowledge of, seeing as the cartoon was on air in the 1960's. "There's plenty more where that came from if you guys can show me good behaviour!" he shouted at them as they frolicked towards the trees. Mike said, "I'm running out of ideas for activities they can do that doesn't require any more energy from me."

"I hear you, times have been tough," I said in response.

He held out the white bottle to me, offering me a vitamin chewable, as if he was sharing a bag of chips. "I'm good, thanks," I politely declined. I wondered internally, Do they even still make Flintstones vitamins? Or was that bottle severely expired and just happened to be sitting in his cupboard for years? In hindsight, I wish I had asked him these questions. He set the bottle beside him. Mike would toss more Flintstones vitamins to each of his children if they allowed him to sit on the bench in peace. It was like watching someone toss bread crumbs to Canadian Geese from a park bench, but way more undignified. He crossed his arms while watching his kids play. Within a minute, his eyes closed and he fell asleep, sitting upright. Not even that large coffee could keep him awake. As I was looking at his face to see if he was actually sleeping, I noticed that he had tried to shave but missed a large patch of hair on his cheek. Within two minutes, he began to snore.

Twenty minutes went by and I kept an eye on both sets of kids while he napped, the least I could do for this fatigued father. Once his children noticed that he was asleep they forgot all about the pathetic pine cone game and decided to create a new game called "Let's See If We Can Steal The Flintstones Bottle From Dad." Clearly, this wasn't the first time they'd tried to take advantage of Mike's physical and mental state.

They tip-toed through the wood chips like soldiers trying to avoid a minefield, stopping periodically to remove them from their shoes. They reached Mike and silently swiped the bottle from the bench ledge, and then bolted for the street to head home. Mission accomplished. Mike was in a coma. I had to shake his arm to wake him up. "Mike, your kids stole your Flintstones vitamins and are running away" I said with a loud voice. I never thought I'd have to utter a sentence like that.

Mike leapt to his dirty bare feet and ran after them with a gorilla-like sprint, shouting, "Get back here now! You guys are in big trouble!" His statements fell on deaf ears as his kids continued to run. Mike then lost his footing, likely from quickly waking up in a panic, and tripped in the wood chips, rolling in a sort of demented somersault. He let out a few loud expletives before getting up and continuing the chase. You could see wood chips clinging to his sweatpants. My own kids watched in amusement from the top of the slide as the fiasco unfolded. My son laughed because Mike's butt crack was now hanging out of his pants as he was in fast pursuit. He yelled to me, "Chase us like that guy, Dad!" my cue for knowing my bench break was over.

I thought I was the "Zombie Dad" that day until I met Mike.

Seven months into it, and the coronavirus is still spreading throughout the world. It isn't just a virus that attacks the lungs and immune system; this virus has been quickly turning parents into the walking dead. Exhaustion, sudden job loss, tending to needs of children 24/7 and ongoing anxiety about the unknown are arguably more dangerous than the virus itself. A horde of weary parents is growing and we may yet have an apocalyptic mental health crisis on our hands.

If only the cure to fix burnout like this was a bottle of Flintstones vitamins, then Mike would be immune.

ABOUT THE AUTHOR

Dallas wrote his first book on the couch next to his aquarium during the COVID-19 pandemic. Mandatory isolation resulted in him having an epiphany that he could do something besides working from home all day and watching Netflix all evening.

He has spent the last 10 years doing a combination of ministry, elementary teaching and psychotherapy. These are professions that helped him hone his storytelling abilities. He's written a lot over the years, having degrees and interests in history, religious studies, education and psychology but this was largely dry academic papers that even he wouldn't want to read again.

Growing up in Winnipeg, Manitoba is something he's insanely proud of and is likely where he developed his bizarre sense of humour, a side effect of the frigid weather on his brain. He credits his grandfather for modelling how to tell a good story that makes people laugh, his main goal in publishing his first book.

If Dallas isn't doing therapy or writing, he's probably hanging out with his beautiful British wife Hannah and two awesome sons, Micah and Luke.

Follow Dallas on Social Media:

www.facebook.com/dallastpublishing

Made in the USA
Monee, IL
06 December 2020

51284827R00066